PASS THE TORCH

PASS THE TORCH

A Rallying Call to Rescue the Future of Trades

MANJA HORNER

To request permissions, contact the publisher at
jennifer@entouragemedia.ca.

Editing: Jennifer Goulden
Editing and Interior Design: Chris Arnold
Cover Design: Mary Luna

ISBN (Hardcover): 978–1–0696618–7–6
ISBN (Paperback): 978–1–0696618–8–3
ISBN (e-Book): 978–1–0696618–9–0
ISBN (Audiobook): 978–1–996848–00–5
First Edition Printed in Canada: March 2026
1 2 3 4 5 6 7 8 9 10

ENTOURAGE
...

Published by Entourage Media
entouragemedia.ca

To Dane, Livi, Gemma, and Edison,
for their support in helping me find the time to write this book
at all hours of the day.

To all of the brilliant men and women: mentors in my life
who took the time to pass me their torch.

CONTENTS

INTRODUCTION

"What the frick are those idiots doing?!" I stopped dead. My dad and I were outside the cafe where we'd just had lunch. He followed my stare across the street to the scene unfolding on the scaffolding—a scene that, in our family, could only be described as a crime.

I covered my mouth to keep from breathing in the red dust that drifted through the air and settled on the vehicles lining the street, including my freshly washed F150. The entire block had a thin layer of red dust coating everything. I looked at my dad with a *"what the heck"* look on my face. He just clenched his teeth, jaw muscle pulsing, and shook his head in that familiar British way of his. I knew what he was thinking, too.

Scaffolding had been erected on a prominent red brick building. As a history nerd, active in our Architectural Conservancy (ACO) group and daughter of a heritage contractor, I knew about it. It was a late-1800s building that had served as a luxury hotel for travelers coming from Rochester, NY, across Lake Ontario to Cobourg, ON.

Two workers stood on the unwrapped scaffolding with evil-looking grinders, attempting to remove the peeling, aged paint from that historic facade. Their method of paint removal was appalling.

"The way they are removing that lead-based paint shouldn't be allowed," Dad said.

My mouth went dry at the thought of the irreversible damage done to something so valuable to a town that tries to preserve its heritage elements. The rough sanding and grinding of the bricks exposed them to the elements and risked the masonry's structural integrity.

"You can see the gouges and grooves from here! How does this happen?" I asked the question mostly out of frustration. I already knew the answer. It's a problem at many job sites.

Poor work is not always the result of crews that don't care. It is frequently caused by awarding contracts to the lowest bidder, and we don't have a policy or enforcement to guarantee that a qualified workforce gets the job. It is almost guaranteed that the tradespeople on this site weren't properly trained to work on buildings like these. New construction calls for different skills than repair, maintenance, or restoration. So, here we are, watching a noble heritage building bleed tears of brick dust, at the mercy of people who don't know how to do any better.

That's when realization dawned on me. I turned to my dad and said, "We should do something about this." I've always believed that if you aren't happy with something, you should do something about it. "We are actually people who can do something about this." At this point in my life, I had a booming career in training development, knowledge of skilled trades, and a subject-matter expert standing right beside me.

With my training background and dad's 30 years of carpentry and restoration experience, we could create training programs for the industry that would help prevent disasters like the one before us from ever happening again. That building didn't have a voice to protect itself, and that untrained, low-budget crew had most likely been set up to fail. My mind started spinning, filled with ideas and solutions to a problem that I knew ran through the entire trades industry. A fire sparked in my belly that afternoon.

I was used to moving fast. I had a unique education as a kid. I was homeschooled before homeschooling was popular. In the '90s, only hippies and oddballs were homeschooling their children (sorry, hippies and oddballs). For me, I'm grateful. This was the best possible way to start my education. I thrived with independence and autonomy, and I got to do some unconventional things.

It gave me time to learn the violin from a young age, and I started teaching music in my teens, helping others develop their own skills.

I got to help my dad in his construction business, doing bookkeeping and data entry behind the scenes.

And, I got to work in the shop, using power tools. Turning spindles and decorative elements on the lathe. Tinkering with hand tools and scraps of exotic wood—observing and learning without getting in the way.

Working for dad, I learned, while high up on a scaffold, how to solder copper flashing and strip layers of peeling and cracking paint to reveal the original old lumber beneath. With care, we would revitalize old wood and prepare it for new finishes. It was a time of sweating in Tyvek protective suits, working with both old and new methods to get a superior, lasting result, thinking critically, and, oh yeah, having no fingerprints after using sandpaper for months on end!

I had a unique position among the crew as "the boss's daughter," working alongside a smaller crew of other young women, my sisters, and some girlfriends. We all learned to treat 150-year-old wood with finesse and care, putting in a level of detail on a third-story window that would never be appreciated from the ground.

Woodwork restoration project on a heritage home. I recall that I had no fingerprints from stripping and sanding after months on the job.

My dad is a perfectionist. I remember on a one-of-a-kind copper-and-cedar roof project, he demanded a perfectly finished copper edge (the edge tucked under cedar shingles). We questioned the necessity of this. His response was, "In 100 years, when someone opens this up and sees my name etched in there, I want them to be awed at the work we did."

I worked alongside characters, mainly immigrant men from Europe and the UK who learned their trade through apprenticeships, hard work, experimentation, and trial and error. Even if I didn't fully appreciate it at the time, I now feel privileged to have gained those insights, tips, and hands-on skills.

My first time on an all girls crew, in a tyvek suit restoring this heritage home after a devastating fire.

I used to love sitting around the dinner table with my dad, hearing stories from the job site. I helped him in the evenings with bookkeeping and data entry for over 10 years. I absorbed all I could. He vented about client and business problems: pricing, budget concerns, delays in accounts receivable, and other challenges of entrepreneurship. I heard firsthand the real and gritty difficulty that comes with apprenticeship programs and dealing with the government through taxes and payroll. Nothing in my university business degree would come close to what I experienced with my sleeves rolled up within the family business.

Looking back, I was a prime candidate to go into the trades, but in those days, students with good grades were funneled into university, not trade school. This was a common reality at the turn of the millennium.

After high school, and in between my other jobs, I squeezed in two university degrees: first in business and then in education. After school, I spent a few years in a corporate job where I developed training programs and learned everything I could in the most professional settings.

Our crew spent five months working on exterior restoration, painting, copper, and woodwork.
Photo: Barbara Raué

My amazing corporate bosses had me developing a high volume of training in topics like leadership, coaching, skill development, communications, and other human-related topics. Because of my background in music teaching, I knew how to develop skills through training. I thought practically. I focused on developing skills in my fellow employees through practice and on-the-job application. I was obsessed with making people's jobs easier by using intuitive resources that would help them do their job better.

Eventually, I left the corporate gig and started freelancing as a curriculum developer for companies in various industries. Trucking along, working for myself, I developed training for topics including manufacturing and blue-collar safety, technical skills, leadership, communications, medicine, pharmacy, sales, and more. I joke that I collect mini PhDs every time I develop a new course.

At first, I didn't even consider developing training systems for the trades industry because sometimes you don't even see what is right in front of you. I had a depth of understanding that I didn't even realize was valuable. As my career expanded, I kept thinking of the many teenage summers I spent working for Dad's company—sweaty, dirty, and doing laborer tasks on prominent heritage buildings—and how much I loved it and learned from it.

Since then, I've watched the domino effect of long-time mentors and experts within the trades retiring before passing a generation's worth of knowledge and expertise on to the next generation workforce. In recent years, I have developed a brand-new mission for my professional life–training the next generation of skilled workers. Part of that mission is to solve the problems we're all sensing in the skilled trades and manufacturing workforce:

- Capture knowledge from the wise old guys—the trades masters and veterans of job sites—before they all retire.
- Train people way faster to fill the looming skilled worker gap.
- Attract the next generation to the trades.
- Make workplaces amazing to work at.
- Help tradespeople become incredible leaders.

A Sense of Obligation

Working for my dad was informative in so many ways. His general contracting firm specialized in historic restoration: replication of wood components, coordinating brick, plaster, and stone masonry restoration, glass, and even metal restoration and preservation. It taught me to love the craft methods and skills involved in repairing beautiful things that many people take for granted. I can't imagine a world in which these trades aren't alive and thriving. I want a new generation of workers to pick up this torch before it's too late.

I am fueled by an urgency to capture the wisdom and methods of our experts, our senior craftspeople, before they leave the industry for good—so much so that I've built a company around it.

We are fully aware of the vast experience and knowledge that will retire with the boomers if we don't find a way to pass it down. We know there are fewer Gen Xers (born between

1965 and 1980) and millennials (born between 1983 and 1994) in the worker pool, yet the heavy burden of leadership and training is landing on their shoulders. We also know there are loads of young workers who are new to the industry who think, learn, and expect VERY different workplaces than the generations only slightly older than themselves.

We are being called to capture the wisdom and practices of your expert staff and help to pass it on through training and digital knowledge banks.

We're being asked to develop training that builds skills faster—we don't have years to waste.

We're being asked to meet the next generation of workers where they're at and help companies train and create workplaces that give younger generations what they crave: respect and purpose.

As an entrepreneur myself, I understand what's driving companies.

In booming industries like manufacturing and skilled trades, company owners want to scale and meet demand. They want to build big enough to meet market demand and live a comfortable lifestyle or leave a legacy. Across the industry, they're struggling to recruit and retain enough skilled workers to make their goals possible.

Hiring and recruiting have become a generational battle. Almost every plant, factory, trades company, and many union halls say they can't find good people. If you talk to leaders in the trades, they'll tell you:

- Older workers are retiring, and there's no one to step into their shoes.

- The new generation expects too much.
- Young people don't have common sense and don't know what they're doing.
- Supervisors can't seem to think for themselves or plan ahead, which causes losses in profit.
- Apprentices take way too long to be productive members of the crew.
- Apprentices are going to leave, so why bother investing in them?

But there's so much more to it than meets the eye. And all of these things are fixable.

We are missing opportunities staring us in the face, and it's costing us millions in turnover, rework, delays, training gaps, and burnout.

My vision for my impact in the industry is laser-fucking-focused on helping tradespeople win. Most skilled-trades leaders are, first and foremost, tradespeople. They are not often businesspeople. They probably went to trade school, not business school. They are welders, masons, and construction contractors; barbers, hairdressers, and chefs; general machinists and carpenters. They've maybe stumbled into leadership or ownership out of a desire to grow their career, work for themselves, or carve their own piece of ownership in the market without ever really having much help with the business or training side of things along the way.

My company, Boost, works with leaders every day to help manage the people side of their businesses, and in this book, I open up my thought process and toolkit and share it for the first time. I'll show you how to make onboarding programs and employee training, retain people and develop their skills faster. I'll reveal why and how to train leaders and supervisors. I argue for the value in creating apprenticeship programs and career development pathways. I'll share with you how to set up cutting-edge technology to help you future-proof your systems. And, of course, I'll show you how to recruit great people.

Knowing trades so deeply, I always make sure what I'm recommending is practical and useful. I know my recommendations have to directly impact a job well done.

Throughout this book, I will force you to look in the mirror and challenge your own perceptions. Then I'll give you the systems we use with our clients to save them money and make them great places to work.

I want you to be successful. I want you to beat your competition, not by being the lowest bidder on a contract, but by having the best workers in the industry, all of whom have been trained with your expertise and methods. I want other companies to be jealous of your workforce. I want you to raise the bar across your industry so that others will pop their head over your fence and copy what you're doing.

Anyone with a toolbelt is standing at a crossroads right now, including me. As a third-generation tradesperson, choosing the right path from here, for the trades, has become my mission in life and work. It has led me back home to where it all began.

In times of distress, we're called to rally and take action. The time to take action is *now*, and *we* are the ones who have to take it—the business owners and leaders, union leaders, trainers, and tradespeople. We're the generation perfectly positioned to either watch our industry fall before our eyes or to take action and watch it thrive. We are the ones who are best able to pass the torch by facilitating the sharing of generations of knowledge and best practices with the new generation of workers. *We* are the ones to get out of this skilled worker and labor market crisis. Let me show you how we're going to do it.

CHAPTER 1

THE DISTRESS SIGNAL

Don't Look—We're Doing Fine . . . It's All Fine!

NORTH AMERICA IS SITTING UNDER A CLOUD OF ECONOMIC and political discouragement at the moment.

Housing starts are a strong indicator of economic health. Taxes in many places are so high that housing affordability is a real issue. Why is it so expensive? In Ontario, 36 percent of the cost of a new house is going toward taxes at various levels of government. Developers aren't building at the same rates because no one can afford to buy after the post-COVID price surges.

Politics are tumultuous and impacting building and manufacturing. Tariffs on materials threaten to impact investment in major projects. Questions around trade agreements mean shipping raw and finished goods is complicated and expensive. Infrastructure projects are propping up the construction sector, funded by governments going deeper into debt.

News headlines are trying to encourage us, splashing words like pipelines, data centers, immigration, and housing starts, yet they aren't telling the whole story. They're placating the public into thinking that everything is okay. Investors and industry leaders know differently.

Generation Z, those born between 1995 and 2006 (who should be full of optimism), do not believe they will ever be able to own a home. They're putting off having families because they're adding up the cost to raise kids, and they don't think it will be possible. They're not wrong. Cost of living increases and housing prices are forcing the workforce to demand much more from their employers.

Employers are feeling the pressure to pay more from every angle.

Demand Isn't Slowing Down

Despite the challenges and affordability, demand in housing, industrial, commercial, infrastructure (ICI), and manufacturing is all high.

During and after the pandemic, we saw mass relocations, putting pressure on housing inventory. Migration is changing the social fabric and housing needs. We need more houses built, and we need different types of housing to accommodate families' changing needs and lifestyles. Even though people can't easily buy, we still need places for people to live.

The demand for new construction in industrial, commercial, and infrastructure sectors paints a less dismal future. Power plants and data centers need to be built. Nuclear energy is having a boom and will be pulling trades resources to build reactors over the next 25 years. This is prime time for people who know how to build. If you're in the business of producing and constructing, my friend, you are sitting in a great position, and you know it.

And it's not all about the bright and shiny new builds. North America's age is showing. Demand for repair and renovation is arguably higher than new construction. There are hundreds of thousands of buildings on the heritage registers in North America. These buildings are well over 100 years old. That number doesn't include every residential, industrial, and commercial building over the age of 100 that is *not* on the register. In fact, 38.4 percent of all pre-1941 dwellings are in need of major repair. Preserving these structures takes special treatment by specialized tradespeople. Skills to build new are different from skills to repair across every industry.

City and town infrastructure across North America is crumbling. Look anywhere, and you'll see deteriorated roads, crumbling concrete, aging bridges, and outdated watermains and sewers. Much infrastructure is past its design life and urgently in need of repair or replacement. In the US and Canada, utilities report about 260,000 water main breaks annually, costing an estimated $2.6 billion USD in direct and indirect repair costs. An estimated 19 percent of installed water mains are considered beyond their useful life and in dire need of replacement. That's roughly 452,000 miles of pipe to fix!

The sheer volume of failing water infrastructure alone implies countless jobs in pipe renewal, trenching, repaving, and associated structural repair. The list of capital renewal needs has become overwhelming.

"Construction is a key contributor to Canada's economic

output, accounting for seven percent of our national gross domestic product, and employing 1.6 million people, or about one in every 13 working Canadians," says Sean Strickland, Chair of BuildForce Canada and President of Canada's Building Trades Unions.

He goes on to say that labor-force pressures are created by growing demand for construction activity and the imminent retirement of older, experienced workers.

The Comeback Tour

Despite the challenges and uncertainty, demand is strong. The need to build and fix is growing by the year. This provides an incredible opportunity for skilled people with common sense and practical ability. The demand for people who can do the work needed is monumental. For people willing to learn and work in the trades, the work will be there for them.

In online trends, the pendulum is swinging back toward nostalgia and "the way things were." Sections of the population remember when things were better, more beautiful, and people had more practical skills. I believe parents are worried about losing hands-on skills with the next generation, so they're waking up and reintroducing practical activities into their homes. They're worried that kids are better at playing video games than they are at handling practical, real-life situations.

Digital content creators are introducing a younger generation to hands-on hobbies and crafts in a new way. A new generation is gardening, making sourdough bread, cooking, sewing, blacksmithing, woodworking, hair cutting, and barbering. For millions of young people, they're craving the tangible.

Business influencers are jumping on the opportunity. They're alerting young people to a disturbing fact. Profitable trades businesses are closing with no one wanting to take over. They're advising and teaching young people about the opportunity to buy boring businesses from a silver wave of retirees. They're positioning small main-street businesses and skilled trades businesses as sure bets for the future, a hedge against Artificial Intelligence (AI) taking their jobs.

Governments are also paying attention and investing. They're spending money to recruit youth into apprenticeships. They're providing grants for skill development and training in the trades. Crumbling infrastructure is getting money for repair and restoration. Federally funded infrastructure projects are keeping the building economy stimulated during residential uncertainty.

It's not just about funding. A shift is taking place in education toward the perception of blue-collar apprenticeships and skilled trades as smart career options. Young people are being presented with trades as a way to start making money right out of high school, rather than racking up student loan debt from colleges and universities.

The trades are having their great comeback moment. Maybe not as big as Guns N' Roses' $500 million comeback tour, but arguably with less plastic surgery and arthritis.

Trades appear to have become our communal safety blanket—for good reason. Skilled trades feel protected for now from the AI and technology disruption that is barreling toward us like a tidal wave. It feels safe to see young people returning to skilled trades as a career choice and to see the pendulum swing back to reclaiming hands-on work as a badge of pride.

Is It Too Little Too Late?

A steady demand for new construction and repair is promising for the economy and awesome if you're a worker in hot demand, but frustrating if you're in charge of hiring! Where the heck are we going to find skilled people to get all this work done?

We've been in a skilled worker recruitment shortage for years. Now there's a rising demand to increase the overall size of the skilled trades workforce to keep up with future staffing needs by 2033.

Employers are fishing from a shrinking pond of experienced workers.

So, we're recruiting, but has this recruitment effort started too late?

Even with the improving social perception toward careers in dirty jobs, increased immigration, and increased government investment in apprenticeship and trades education, we have a major skilled labor shortage today, and it's about to get worse.

A looming wave of retirement is about to compound the problem.

One in five skilled trades workers is over the age of 55. Bless this generation. They've worked so hard. They're no doubt tired from working hard over 30-40-year careers, and they're looking forward to what's next.

Not only are we looking at staggering retirement numbers, but we're seeing a massive brain drain of expertise preparing to age out when they drive away from the jobsite for the last time. These hard workers have gained a lot of experience over a long period of time. They started young and have worked in factories and on jobsites, working loyally for decades.

It's hard to get accurate numbers across North America because skilled trades are needed across many industries with hundreds of different roles and job titles. Despite this, the estimated numbers in Canada and the United States are staggering. Leading into 2033, roughly one in five workers is expected to retire, largely baby boomers aging out of the trades.

In Canada, 700,000 of the approximately four million skilled tradespeople are set to retire. Even with an effort to recruit to fill that gap, we expect to be left short by at least 150,000 skilled tradespeople in 2033.

In the United States, retirement statistics are similar, but population size magnifies the issue. Based on projections, skilled trades and manufacturing industries anticipate that two to three million skilled trades and manufacturing jobs will go unfilled by 2033.

The retirement wave isn't just coming; it's already reshaping the workforce.

Not only are we losing the head count, but we're also losing decades of experience and mastery. "Ontario is losing a generation of craft mastery," said David Piccini, Ontario

Minister of Labour, Immigration, Training and Skills Development. "We're exploring ways to re-engage retirees as teachers and mentors, so that employers and apprentices alike don't lose decades of experience."

These shocking numbers of retirement and high-paying skilled jobs that were soon to be left unfilled were my wake-up call.

Maybe this attention to the statistics that are easy to track was the reality check that we all needed?

Wanted: Trained and Skilled People–Available to Start Yesterday!

Millions of skilled workers needed . . . A mass exodus of retiring tradies . . . *Oh shit!* We have an 8-year runway to recruit, train, and certify millions of people in highly regulated industries.

The average person is feeling the shortage of experienced workers. Just think of the last time you tried to find a decent plumber on short notice. Try hiring someone to replace a pane of glass in your heritage window, find a piano tuner in your small town, get started on your home addition, or get your bicycle repaired by someone who actually knows what they're doing. Good luck finding someone on short notice. Skilled people are stretched thin and are in hot demand.

These are remnants from lackluster recruitment efforts over 20 years ago. We have good people, just not enough of them.

It's fine that the industry is now madly scrambling to recruit young people to the trades. The problem is that you don't create a trained and certified worker in two years. We need skilled people who actually know what they're doing—trained and certified to work, not just warm bodies standing around pushing brooms and carrying heavy things.

Recruiting new people is only one part of the solution. Narrowly focusing on unskilled newcomers is like thinking you can solve your company's cash flow problem this week by running some ads. No . . . it takes time for those ads to turn into leads and then dollars in your bank account. It's not a quick fix; it's a long-term strategy, and you may not survive bankruptcy. You should have read the signs before the cash ran out and done something proactively.

Recruitment efforts are attracting curious high schoolers who are interested in getting into the trades. Based on where we're at with recruiting and promoting trades for young people, my outlook for the future is bright . . . 15 years from now.

This focus on active recruitment is bringing in new apprentices in decent numbers. The health of the top of the recruitment pipeline is improving. In fact, apprenticeship enrollment is over double today compared to the mid-1990s in Canada. In 1994, there were approximately 160,000 apprentices enrolling, according to Statistics Canada. In 2023, we had 460,000 apprentices enrolled in skilled trades.

In the US, apprenticeship enrollment efforts are making headway as well. Active apprenticeships increased by 35 percent since the early 2000s. But apprenticeship completions across the board are only about 50 percent, another problem we will talk about later. Recruitment and apprenticeship enrollment are improving, but those things are not solving our immediate need for skilled workers and generating skills and experience quickly.

The Worker Pipeline

A worker pipeline (often called a talent or recruitment pipeline) is a structured, ongoing strategy for identifying, engaging, and nurturing strong candidates before positions open up. Instead of waiting for someone to quit and then scrambling to find a replacement (reactive hiring), a company with a pipeline has a ready-to-use "pipe" filled with qualified, pre-vetted candidates.

You never want to stop filling the top of the pipeline with new people. Then, you need to move people through the pipeline. You need to nurture and build that workforce once they're in the pipeline, until they're a strong and capable craftsperson, tradesperson, journeyperson, supervisor, and foreman.

Worker Pipeline

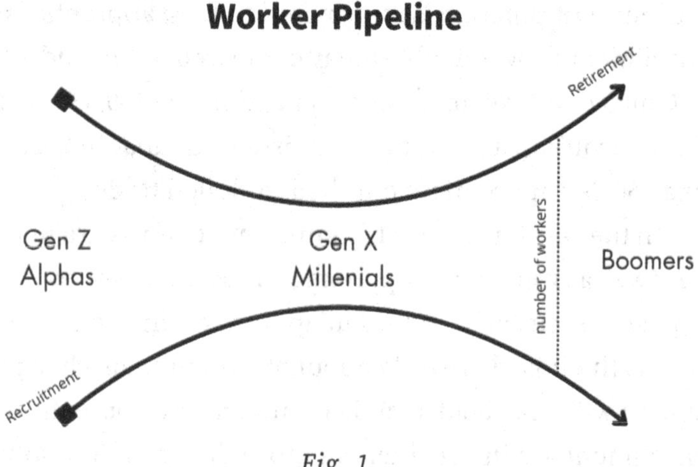

Fig. 1

This worker pipeline image (*see Fig. 1*) shows how the workforce pipeline has a squeezed middle. Lots of Gen Z and Alpha are entering the workforce on one end, and lots of boomers are leaving the workforce on the other. In the middle, we see the result of 40 years of lackluster recruitment into the trades. With boomers leaving their experienced leadership roles, the Gen Xers and millennials, poised to be the top dogs in the workforce, don't exist in a balanced volume to lead and train a large influx of recruits and untrained newcomers.

Many trades have a 1:1 ratio of journeyperson to apprentice. We can't train the volume of apprentices needed if this is the case.

While it's great that we have a volume of people making their way into the trades, working with trades leaders across industries, here are the challenges still looming beyond recruitment:

- Keeping mid-career tradespeople and small employers engaged as mentors and leaders.
- Incentivizing employers to take on apprentices.
- Modernizing apprenticeship training so it's more suitable for the volume needed and the learning style of today's workforce.
- Updating apprenticeship regulations, including standards, ratios, and paperwork requirements.
- Getting companies on board so they're not just complaining about the gap in experience, but they're also investing in training their own workers.
- Creating safe and enjoyable workplaces that retain

new-to-role workers, including women, young people, and apprentices.

Market uncertainty and frustrations with hiring new unskilled people make employers hesitant to hire and train. Companies want to hire ready-to-go people. But they're all recruiting from a shrinking talent pool, so it's getting harder to find ready-to-go talent.

Sure, it's more comfortable to hope someone else will fix the problem rather than doing it ourselves, but that's not an option for a future-ready leader.

Immigration is One Way To Solve the Problem

What do we do historically when we don't have the people to meet demand? We look to the rest of the world and try to bring them in. North America is built on immigrants who brought skills to the country and worked hard to make a life for themselves. Growing up, I knew that some of the best skilled tradespeople were immigrants. They came from "the old country." I heard this phrase a lot and appreciate what immigration has done for Canada.

Between the 1950s and 1970s, Canada welcomed tens of thousands of tradespeople, mainly from across Europe, to fill post-war labor gaps. Post-war immigration policy was designed to attract hands-on workers. Nearly nine in ten newcomers became wage earners, and a remarkable share went into manufacturing and construction. These were people who could arrive, start working the next day, and find their footing in the middle class. My grandparents arrived in Canada from

England and Holland around 1959 in exactly this way, finding their way into steel manufacturing and electrical estimating.

FAMILY OF INDUSTRIES .... Representatives of Port Hope industries who attended the dinner given by the Industrial Commission at Greenwood Tower Motel last night. Included are Tim Ottink of Esco Ltd.; Jack Laurie of Mathew's Conveyer and Al Henderson of Nicholson File Ltd.

My grandfather Tim Ottink as plant manager of Esco Steel Casting plant, 16 years after immigrating to Canada.

Immigration has always been a part of the story of skilled trades, but the tone and politics surrounding it have changed dramatically over the last few decades. Where post-war Canada once celebrated the arrival of highly skilled workers like bricklayers, masons, and carpenters who could buy homes, work hard, send their kids to good schools, and thrive without government support, today the system is more complicated and politically charged.

Public attitudes toward immigration have shifted, too. In 2023, an Environics poll found that 46 percent of Canadians believe immigration levels are too high—up 15 percent from a decade ago—even as 78 percent of construction employers report difficulty hiring skilled labor. The contradiction is that we need immigration more than ever.

Immigration used to represent opportunity and craftsmanship; now it sparks tension. We still need immigration to fill the skilled worker shortage; however, we need an immigration policy that supports finding and integrating people who can fill skill gaps properly.

In Canada, tension around this topic comes from how the Temporary Foreign Worker Program (TFWP) operates. It was designed to fill labor shortages but is increasingly criticized for undercutting wages and creating resentment among local workers. Critics argue that the program allows employers to sidestep apprenticeship commitments and exploit short-term labor solutions, while supporters say it keeps projects moving amid chronic shortages.

This is where the politics get personal. The people I meet in trades halls and industry events talk about it off the record and tell me how they really feel. Most aren't angry at immigrants; they're angry at the system.

The challenge runs beyond pay. Many new arrivals come from countries where training systems and safety standards differ significantly from those in North America. Workers from the Philippines, India, and Latin America often bring experience and work effort, but may need time to meet Canadian trade qualifications and regulated safety standards.

In the US, crackdowns on illegal immigration, deportations, and visa restrictions have caused uncertainty in sectors that rely on immigrant labor, threatening to choke off the workforce keeping projects alive. Today, immigrants make up about 30 percent of the US construction workforce, and in states like Texas and California, that number exceeds 40 percent (US Bureau of Labor Statistics, 2024).

For both Canada and the United States, numbers aren't the only issue; it's also about values. Are we welcoming workers as equal contributors? Are we providing training, excellent wages, and career opportunities? Or are we treating people as temporary stopgaps in competition with locals? The politics of immigration is a tricky one to navigate as an employer and leader.

Immigration, once viewed as a solution to the problem of skilled worker shortages, has become a symbol of unease. We need to balance protecting wages, welcoming new talent, maintaining standards, and training the incoming workforce while recognizing the skills they may bring, which we can learn from.

When I asked Piccini, Ontario's Minister of Labour, Immigration, Training and Skills Development, what he envisions for the next decade, he told me:

"Ten years from now, I want an Ontario where every apprentice matters—especially those working with small employers. Every single training agreement counts."

This message is that a consistent and individual focus from small companies to the large ones might be the bridge we need. Every worker counts.

Women Are An Untapped Resource

As a woman in the trades, I vividly remember working on jobsites when I was a teenager. It was fun, albeit grueling at times. I was optimistic, and thankfully, I never felt unsafe or disrespected. I learned to be assertive and valued what I was learning from the guys. My dad loved having female crews because we were attentive to detail, worked quickly, and brought a different perspective to the work.

Women might be the greatest source of untapped potential in manufacturing and skilled trades. But things have to shift, or women will not be attracted to jobs in the trades.

I make a point of talking to women whenever I am on a jobsite, at a conference, or attending a union or trade show event. I want to hear, in their own words, what they experience. I want to know what they are dealing with on a day-to-day basis. How much do they love their jobs?

Many women really enjoy their work, and they find it fulfilling. When I ask them about the common barriers, they're forthcoming. They find long working days and inflexible working conditions and environments to be a challenge, especially for women with children. They want help setting boundaries and being assertive with their male coworkers.

They express that it can feel isolating to be the only woman on the crew. There can be a lack of mentoring and sponsorship as well, so they must work extra hard to prove themselves worthy and able. Many of them feel they have to do way more than men to prove themselves, fit in, and be accepted.

Some skilled trades attract a higher percentage of women, such as hairdressing, chef/cooking, and in decor trades like painting and wallpapering. In many of the other building trades, the percentage of women employed versus men is very low.

In Canada, five percent of apprentices are women based

on the total registrations for construction, manufacturing, and transportation trades. Women in Canada also have a lower completion rate for their apprenticeships; 35 percent of women complete apprenticeships compared to 47 percent completion for men.

In the US, women represent 5-10 percent of the construction workforce. Similar to other countries, the high end of this percentage is from women in occupations such as office, business, financial operations, and sales roles. Similar to Canada, only about five percent of women are in production and construction.

Looking outside of North America, among all working women in India, 5.5 percent work in construction or skilled trades. They're in jobs like masonry, plumbing, or electrical work. Women make up a much smaller share of the skilled trades workforce, and most of those who do work in construction are in lower-paid, informal roles rather than in higher-skilled positions.

In the Philippines, women make up two percent of the construction and skilled trades workforce. There are groups there working to change that by training and organizing women to become carpenters, welders, and builders. Despite progress, most women in these jobs still face bias, limited opportunities, and a lack of recognition for their skills.

I know the challenges and hard work required for a career in the trades. I also know that women are more than capable. I wish more women felt comfortable getting into trades careers—not only in construction, production, and restoration (which is very satisfying, creative, and detail-oriented), but also in project management, estimating, planning, and leadership. The opportunities are endless.

Ownership is also an incredible opportunity for women. I'm networking with more women who have founded and co-founded trades companies in plumbing, HVAC, glazing, and energy companies. Ladies, there are tons of opportunities for us!

I often reflect on my own career. Although I really enjoyed working for those few short years learning restoration, I wasn't encouraged to pursue a full-fledged career in the trades. Not from my guidance counselor, teachers, society, or even my own family. How different would these skilled worker statistics look if we recruited women and cultivated welcoming workplaces?

Culture Isn't a Bad Word–I Swear!

By 2030, millennials and Gen Zers are projected to make up 74 percent of the global workforce, positioning these two cohorts as the dominant influence on workplace culture, values, and expectations.

In North America, immigration, social norms, and these dominant generations are already changing the nature of workplace culture.

Culture isn't a dirty word—I can almost hear your eyes rolling. I know it's scoffed at, but hear me out . . .

Workplace culture refers to all of the ways that people interact on the job. It's the shared behaviors and attitudes, the ways conflict is handled, the way leaders and supervisors interact with employees, and the policies and expectations of what's acceptable. Culture is going to be made with, or without you, so you might as well be intentional about making the one you want.

You will either create a safe and enjoyable culture where people want to stay or a workplace that's tense and unhappy where people can't wait to leave.

Trades are notorious for being a rougher environment. Catcalling, swearing, inappropriate jokes, and a strong drinking culture—all of these stereotypes come from reality. These kinds of workplace behaviors aren't as acceptable today.

Young people in manufacturing and trades, especially women, want different workplace cultures. They want a welcoming workplace that considers well-being and camaraderie, not one that intimidates or makes them feel unsafe.

They also want their career to progress quickly.

Gen Z has the shortest tenure of any generation, switching jobs every 1.1 years according to several studies. They're moving jobs because of a need for higher pay, ambition, and a lack of clear pathways toward career growth. Forty-one percent of Gen Z report that they always consider long-term goals when making job decisions. This is higher than any other generation before them.

Gen Zers want their employers to onboard them well and show them from the start that there is a promising future for them at the company. They want to see that there is a future beyond digging holes and holding a shovel.

The cost of living is so high today that they're looking for great pay, benefits, and flexibility in their jobs, and they're not willing to wait 15 years to get these perks. They expect them from the start.

Gen Zers and millennials are focused on work-life balance as much as learning and development. Making money is important to them, but so is finding meaningful work and well-being.

News flash: this means young people want a different workplace dynamic. They don't want to be yelled at. They won't stick around under those kinds of conditions. Millennials and Gen Zers are taking over the workforce, and they see the world differently. They're not motivated by the same things as previous generations, and they're not loyal enough to put up with any crap.

They want balance, meaning, and a voice at the table. They want to build companies where mental health isn't a joke, where leadership listens, and where the work actually matters. They're not interested in burning themselves out. And they want to be talked to differently.

Jed, a training coordinator for a West Coast trades union, told me: "The guys express challenging communication either in silence or in rage. The yelling might get quick results, but it's not effective over the long term."

Expectations of the millennial and Gen Z generations are vastly different from what boomers and Gen Xers were willing to put up with. Gen Xers were basically ignored by their parents, left to fend for themselves, play on metal playgrounds, and ride their bikes without helmets. They got yelled at and took it out in their rock and punk music. Things were different between 1965 and 1980.

It doesn't mean the younger generations are soft or "need to toughen up." It means we need to lead with more dignity.

The trouble is that some of the generation in leadership

don't have the training or awareness to give younger generations what they need, especially in the way they communicate. They need help to develop new skills in leadership and communication so they can create workplaces that young people want to join and will stay in the long term.

As a Trainer, I'm Rubbing My Hands with Glee

Truthfully, I couldn't be happier to be a training company at this juncture in the industry. We are facing the perfect storm of supply and demand when it comes to the skilled workforce. We have an impatient, untrained, unskilled group of young people who are curious about the trades and willing to explore a job that's safe from AI takeover. We have unions and companies that want to hire workers and get them trained as fast as possible. And we have a world of expertise within a generation that is about to retire before they pass their knowledge on.

Great news for me.

Bad news is that training is often the first investment to be cut because it's hard to tie directly back to revenue and "the bottom line." It feels obligatory and boring. More like a hassle than anything.

News flash! You think you're in the HVAC/Plumbing/Electrical business, but you're not. You're in the people business. Your business isn't worth shit unless the people working for you are great. And people aren't worth their salt unless they are well-trained. If you already get this, you're already investing in your people. But if you've never had this "aha" moment, then you haven't even been thinking about putting dollars toward training and developing your people . . . maybe until today.

As an owner or leader in this industry, your competitive edge and success are with your people. Investing in people is the ground that keeps a business fertile.

I'm seeing a trend of companies and unions bringing their training in-house to be more agile and train people the way they want them to perform. They're investing hundreds of thousands to millions of dollars into creating world-class, hands-on training.

But training has to look different to meet the needs of companies and workers.

Starting with the top.

You've probably promoted good tradespeople into leadership positions. But supervisors and leaders are not very effective if they haven't learned management and communication skills. It's a whole new job description, and they're untrained. Crews and office staff alike will be unorganized and confused without strong leadership. Bottom line, tradespeople need to learn leadership and communication skills.

Training has to be based on outcomes that employers need—less focused on hours spent and more focused on competency. Leaders don't care how long someone sat in a classroom taking a course or how fancy the virtual reality training was. Leaders care that workers can perform a procedure properly, safely, and without making major mistakes that cost materials or time. At the end of the day, money and reputation matter.

Training has to come out of the classroom and onto the jobsite if we want it to work for the volume of people who need to fill these roles. Training needs to be intentional and easily referenced with video, documented procedures, and checklists. Information needs to be available on the job when it's needed—right in the flow of work. Skills need to be stacked and practiced, drilled as we do in sports and music. It has to be *really* fucking practical.

Pathways through apprenticeships and training to upskill someone through the rest of their career have to be crystal clear. Young people need to see that there's a pathway where they can receive training toward future jobs, or they won't stay. They are restless. We can't change that.

Younger generations need different kinds of training—starting with basic skills. Younger people aren't immersed in hands-on work from a young age like they used to be. Kids aren't tinkering in the workshop with their parents, fixing bicycles and screen doors like they did in the past. Schools don't teach the same kind of skills. Kids learn things on screens, theoretically learning from YouTube and social media. Many of them start their trade never having used a tape measure or a tool.

"A lot of these younger workers also never had someone parent them in work habits or confidence," Jed said. "Construction has to do that now—teach people to show up, care, and build with passion again."

So, our company mentors companies to create a culture of learning that's much different than in the past. "People won't care about your skills until they know you care about them," Jed said, echoing his mentor at Starbucks, Howard Behar. "That's the real secret to faster upskilling. Create a culture that makes people care."

There's a lot about the generations that we can't change. So, let's focus on what we can control.

We can't change the education system quickly. We can't make people parent better. Instead of waiting for these systems to change in order to save us, we have to do what we can and change the way we're operating, leading, and training.

CHAPTER 2

HOW DID WE GET HERE

IF YOU'RE TUNED IN AND LOOKING AROUND, YOU WON'T BE surprised by the highlight reel of what's going on today. Most North Americans can see and feel the changes in infrastructure, culture, and society. Drive around and see aging infrastructure, crumbling mid-70s–brutalist era—concrete commercial buildings, and the newer, poorly constructed homes not even built with the ability to be repaired.

"How the fuck did we get here?"

Centuries ago, beauty ruled. Buildings were masterpieces—detailed works of art built over decades by craftsmen. Castles, giant homes, and stunning public buildings were crafted not only in Europe and the UK, but also in North America. From the '40s to the '70s, these historical masterpiece properties all around North America were torn down and replaced with concrete block and square brick monstrosities. Check the historical society records of your city or town if you want to see when the post office, courthouse, and hotels were removed and parking lots and concrete jungles installed in their place.

Buildings that took decades to construct, with the craftsmanship and skilled labor of previous generations, were demolished without a thought. Somewhere in this process, the perception of skilled-trades craftsmen was also being dismantled.

The decline in perception of trades is a symptom of a much bigger problem that's been going on for over 50 years. Today, we're dealing with the consequences of decades of failure to pay attention and focus on the importance of the skilled trades and pride in craftsmanship excellence.

But what happened?

Why did society stop caring about beauty in our design and architecture?

When did trades stop being a prestigious craft where people took great pride and passion in their work and art?

When did the idea of putting in a hard day's work using your hands lose its credibility?

When did we stop recruiting people into the skilled trades?

Funny you should ask. I'm curious about these questions too. I had to go back long before I was even born to understand the real stepping stones on the path to mediocrity and the skilled-worker shortage we're smack dab in today.

The research I did for this book crystallized my assumptions and had me saying repetitively, "Those little fuckers!" Turns out, society is fully influenced by government funding and messaging, education, and media.

Changes happen where money flows. Decades ago, governments started investing away from trades and building beautiful things and into developing a new and burgeoning economy–technology. Politicians stood at podiums and stated that they were investing in the knowledge economy, planting the seeds into hearts and minds that this was the new way forward. Their dollars spoke loudly.

Bottom line, everything in society since the late 1970s has been driving the population toward computers, information technology (IT), innovation, and the "knowledge economy," which meant funds were not directed toward recruiting skilled trades workers, keeping infrastructure in good repair, and incentivizing employers to maintain healthy worker pipelines. We ended up with this chasm between educated desk workers and work-with-your-hands skilled trades employees.

The Education Shift

Government dollars and policy made quick work to push the workforce toward this new knowledge economy of the '80s. The work-with-your-hands trades and dirty jobs fell out of fashion. Sexier and shinier vocations were in: careers that beeped, booped, connected to the internet, and went public on the stock market. Those were the industries that got attention and funding. The public education system churned its wheels and began spitting out a new kind of worker—one who wore shoulder pads, suits, and pantyhose (maybe not all in that combination).

Government funding, tax incentives, programs, and loans—all were designed to point students firmly toward college and university, finishing with a career behind a desk.

High school Career and Technical Education (CTE) classes were dropped. Shop classes, youth apprenticeships, and automotive classes fizzled out.

When I was in high school, the only students I remember

guidance counselors rounding up for careers in trades were the class-skipping pot smokers who hung around behind the auto shop class on the fringes of the woods. Anyone else with grades over 75 was funneled into college or university without question.

My grandfather Tim Ottink as a young student learning automotive mechanics in high school.

Everything funneled "book-smart kids" away from hands-on careers. It was the "skids" who fell through the cracks and made their way into the trades: kids who couldn't sit still in class, couldn't be bothered to hand in homework, or study for tests. We know now how many kids were just bored and needed something different.

Mathematically gifted or engineering-minded students, artists, and creatives weren't given a chance to explore a passion for building, constructing, carving, or crafting. And, what a bloody shame. Today, there are more unhappy desk workers who fell hook, line, and sinker for the "knowledge track" when they would have been brilliant additions to skilled trades and would have been much happier for it.

The numbers don't lie. From 1980 to 2010, postsecondary enrollment across North America doubled. Guidance counselors' job descriptions and training incentivized them to promote colleges and universities.

A high volume of smart kids stopped building with their hands, and our worker pipeline of millennials and Gen Xers is the direct outcome.

The Status Flip

Back in the 1800s, craftsmanship was highly valued. Master craftsmen held an elevated status in families and society. Parents paid for apprenticeship programs for their sons. Being part of a masterpiece building project gave you status. People returning from WWI knew how to work as a team and have each other's backs. The government invested in public perception by putting veterans on a pedestal as nation builders. Industrial work was tied to patriotism and prosperity. Old pictures of steelworkers on I-beams high above Chicago showed men wearing collared shirts, pleated pants, and knit sweaters to work. Being a tradie meant something special.

When did the plumber's-butt, whistle-calling, rough-around-the-edges, beer-drinking stereotype show up and change the narrative from this post-war group of tradespeople?

The media had a hand to play as it always does,

portraying tradesmen as buffoons with their plumber's crack. It hyper-sexualized, showing sweaty and shirtless men at work calling at women walking by with predatory whistles. Everything from '94 Diet Coke ads to music videos reinforced this message. Tim Allen's character, "Tim the Toolman Taylor," from the '90s sitcom *Home Improvement*, showed blue-collar work as silly and unprofessional. Mike Rowe's show *Dirty Jobs* did a lot to expose people to blue-collar work; however, the term "dirty" still keeps a certain stigma firmly in place.

There are misconceptions that skilled trades are low-skill and low-pay, that people in skilled trades are less smart, and that there are fewer opportunities for career advancement in the trades. If you ask people working in the trades, many will tell you they have felt looked down upon.

The Cultural Decline: From Craftsmanship to Convenience

Have you noticed a trend where everything is more expensive, yet of poorer quality?

Very little is made to last anymore.

People don't seem to be as masterful or as skillful as they were in the past.

People don't seem to be able to do high-quality work as before.

Even common sense doesn't seem to be common anymore.

This cultural decline worries me that we're at risk of losing a lot of good from our past.

Our parents and grandparents had higher expectations

of people and their products, cars, and homes than we do. They could afford to buy quality things. Items were built to be beautiful and fixable. Now, they are more utilitarian and built to be thrown away.

There has been an accelerated decline in hands-on skill and craftsmanship in the last 40 years. People spend more time on computers and devices and less on tangible activities like crafts, hobbies, building, and fixing, so we're losing the skill en masse.

Construction of products has sped up, so things are made faster, but they've been reduced in beauty and quality. Houses are not built to last as long. Entire subdivisions are thrown together in weeks; some houses look like they could be knocked down by a strong wind. Materials are more disposable.

Cars aren't made to last much beyond their 96-month payment plans, and you need a login and a computer to fix them. Our idol—the smartphone—is designed to be replaced with a new model every two years; batteries die, and it's cheaper to buy a new phone than replace the battery.

We used to build intricate, beautifully detailed structures and products. Standard work produced today is boxier, plainer, and less repairable.

Culturally, we've lost a sense of excellence, mastery, and pride in quality. Society demands quick, cheap consumer goods. Instead of solid wood, hand-made, high-quality furniture and fashion, we asked for cheap and cheerful. Big box stores and online stores filled with knockoffs stepped up to produce what the market was looking for.

Vehicles used to be rock-solid steel constructions made in

Detroit and Windsor. Now, they're imported plastic machines. Boy, I do admire the steel, chrome, and fabrication of classic cars. I even sometimes miss the 1979 Ford pickup truck that I grew up with.

Remember your grandparents' appliances from the 1970s that are still running? My stainless steel washer-dryer set that I replace every seven years doesn't hold a candle to Grandma's almond and chrome-colored beauties, reliably swishing laundry in the basement.

This year, I stumbled into an old store in the heart of downtown Portland, Oregon. It was a blast from the past to walk through the dilapidated building filled with Western cowboy boots, hats, clothing, and blankets. They sold Pendleton, a 150-year-old USA-made wool brand. Generations of Pendleton fathers and sons have been fabricating high-quality woolen products. I found vintage woolen pants on a shelf on the second floor, tucked away in the corner. The pants were beautifully tailored with perfect seams and thick fabric. Stroking that fabric, I was struck by what we're willing to accept as merchandise today.

This disposable mindset has even changed our cityscapes.

Funding, regulations, and design ideas promoted demolition. During the "Urban Renewal Program" in 1949, entire swaths of cities were demolished and rebuilt to support postwar housing needs.

The Federal-Aid Highway Act (1956) required the demolition of downtown cores of cities for new highways.

In the 1960s, it was common to demolish entire swaths of heritage buildings at a time. Some absolutely iconic buildings that you may not even be aware of were destroyed, and new development was put in their place. Penn Station in New York City was famously demolished to make way for Madison Square Garden and an office building. Many grand Gilded Era homes were removed along Fifth and Park Avenue in NYC for office buildings. Many heritage structures occupied land that could be redeveloped at a higher profit by erecting larger and taller structures. So, they were removed.

Booming post-war immigration demanded more housing. An active campaign to remove old buildings, changing design standards, and updated building codes meant the old, beautiful buildings weren't treasured, and craftsmanship became expendable.

"The Greeks and Romans built beauty first—and then figured out the math," a trades trainer said. "Now we've flipped it. We're building only what's efficient. We need artists in the trades again—people who build cathedrals, not just walls." I echo this feeling. I'd love to see trades respected as beauty and artistry again.

The Broken Chain Starts At Home

We got into this situation because we stopped passing down the capabilities and skills needed to build, test, explore, and repair from one generation to the next.

On one hand, we have helicopter parents who organize play dates, brush their kids' teeth until they're 10, bubble wrap them at the playground, and wouldn't dream of letting their child use an axe, pocket knife, or saw to build a fort. Heaven forbid Johnny gets hurt! Kids suffer. It's hard to build an independent adult with skills if you never allowed them to do anything as a child.

On the other hand, you've got disengaged parents who may know how to fix a bicycle, build a deck, or re-tile a floor, but they don't pass down their skills to their kids because they're busy or distracted. They break the link in the chain of intergenerational knowledge transfer.

I learned a story that stuck with me. WD-40 was forced to launch an ad campaign aimed at a new generation of kids who weren't familiar with the brand anymore. They hadn't grown up in the garage, greasing their bicycle chain. They haven't helped a parent get the squeak out of hinges using the famous lubricant. So WD-40 launched a "Repair Challenge" to encourage people to use its products and lean into a repair culture. A brand synonymous with fixing things a generation ago now needed a marketing campaign to rebuild awareness.

Instead of tinkering with something until we figure it out, younger generations spend 30 seconds trying, give up, then search YouTube for a demonstration on how it's done. YouTube creators are teaching our kids what we should be teaching them. Kids learn how to change a tire . . . from YouTube. Kids learn how to build Lego after watching 24 hours of videos, for goodness' sake.

It starts with us as parents. Teach your kids how to safely use a pocket knife and a hand tool. Teach them to measure, fix, and build. Show kids how to sew, plan projects, and use power tools to build simple constructions. Let them take apart small engines and electronics to see how they work inside.

We wrongly assume that kids don't want to know what

we know, and that they don't want to work hard or work with their hands. We assume that kids don't want to get dirty and make something. These assumptions are dead wrong.

Profitable Companies Are Disappearing

When kids aren't taught about the value of working in the trades, they miss out on opportunities. Did you know that more than 70 percent of companies will change hands in the next decade? They'll either close up or get sold. Many of these are family businesses in trades that have no exit plan. These are profitable businesses, employing people and providing goods and services to their communities.

Family businesses that started in a garage or with a pickup truck are closing up shop because the owner is ready to fish, travel, or finally spend time with family. Others are being sold off to private equity or quietly fading out when there's no one left to take the reins.

Young people aren't choosing to inherit or buy family businesses. They're heading off into alternate industries. In 2021, 44,000 businesses were abandoned, closing forever. These numbers are mind-blowing.

It's a shame when decades of experience are lost—when the person who can fix anything with ingenuity and minimal resources suddenly isn't there anymore. There are thousands of small and mid-sized trades businesses in which the owner wears all the hats. They're the estimator, the service provider, the trainer, and the guy with all the contacts, and they haven't managed to document anything to pass along their know-how to an up-and-comer.

When someone does show interest in taking over, they have a monumental job of learning how to run things. Why is it so hard for someone new to pick up the torch?

Partly because the generations speak different languages, and the new generation owners ask uncomfortable questions, such as "Why do we do it this way?" "Why isn't this written down?" and "Why are we yelling at people instead of training them?" They're challenging the status quo by introducing technology and flipping things on their head.

Some of the "old guard" are ready to pass the torch. Others are gripping it like a hammer, and they're not done swinging. But the handoff is coming whether they're ready or not. The smart ones will start preparing now. Smart business owners will start capturing what they know, mentoring someone younger, and accepting that legacy isn't about control. It's about continuity.

The way I see it, the last generation built the structures. They built the bridges, the towers, and the buildings. The current generation is going to be responsible for repairing and preserving those buildings, rebuilding the culture of an industry while they're at it.

Look Inside Our Own House

We can't blame everything on postwar housing shortages or profit projects, YouTube, or a lack of old-school parenting. We should consider that the problem likely goes deeper, to the culture we created and the attitudes we normalized.

We have seen a decline in trades enrollment and retention

because there are still issues in our own house that need to be addressed. We have work to do:

- as leaders
- on our culture
- on our work conditions, pay, and job security
- on our training pathways and career opportunities
- and on helping people find purpose and meaning in the work.

I ran a private LinkedIn channel poll and found that of 150 responders, 128 said they had been screamed at on the job. This may have been okay 50 or 60 years ago, but the younger workforce will not accept being yelled at during work.

There are better ways to demand excellence. So, why is this still happening?

The mentality that "I was yelled at, and I turned out fine" persists, perpetuating the cycle. Today's leaders worked on the tools, got yelled at, started supervising, and now lead teams themselves. They pass on what they know—including verbal abuse.

Leaders don't worry about intentionally training people because the old way is to hire cheap and young labor and make them learn by osmosis. Young people don't stick around long enough to learn that way. They have other options.

Fix these issues, and we'll be able to hire well and retain the people we get.

CHAPTER 3

MYTH BUSTING

"Kids these days are lazy."
"Tradies are rednecks."
"Common sense doesn't exist anymore."
"I always have to babysit my crews."
"There are not enough skilled people who want to work."

STEREOTYPES DO EXIST FOR A REASON. I'LL GIVE YOU that. But there are generalizations that are simply not true.

Myth: Young People Aren't Interested in Trades

Society has been cultivated so that it's ripe to set people up for soft-skill jobs, remote work, more comfortable lifestyles, less hands-on hard work, and more passive income. We glorify a "work smart, not hard" mentality. *The 4-Hour Workweek* is 17 years old and still a bestseller.

It's not uncommon to hear about social media sensations making unreal amounts of money. Mr. Beast today has 445 million subscribers and is reported to have a $1 billion net worth. He's one of the richest content creators. Don't try to tell me the kids aren't enthralled by this example. They think they can cash in on this apparent get-rich-quick scheme. Even my six-year-old will tell you with complete confidence that he wants to be a YouTuber when he grows up.

Online influencers give kids everywhere the impression that you simply launch your beauty line, wear the makeup, show up in your perfect, medically crafted body, and you, too, can be living #yourbestlife rolling up to the beach in your Lambo. They elevate easy living and wild wealth, without showing the challenge and hard work that got them there.

And let's face it: The trades do require an element of sacrifice. Manufacturing facilities are noisy, repetitive, and can be dirty. Tradespeople do work harder, lift heavier, and experience more physical discomfort in a day. Tradespeople wear more clothing and protective equipment that's hot in the summer. Tradespeople are more exposed to the elements, where it can be very cold in the winter. The hours can be long, and conditions can be hard on the body.

This doesn't mean young people don't want the work. But we do need to expose younger students to the options and realities of work in the trades. Virtual Reality, Youth Apprenticeship Programs in high school, general college pre-apprenticeships, and summer jobs can give young people exposure to the realities so they can decide for themselves.

Myth: Younger Generations Don't Want What Their Grandparents Had

In a digital age, we may broadly assume that young people don't care about a lifestyle grounded in hands-on skills and "earning an honest living," that they don't want the hard work and long work days that our parents and grandparents had, or that they only want something new and easy.

But it's not true. The beauty of the human experience is that what's old always becomes new again. We're seeing a resurgence toward crafts, trades, skilled work, and an understanding that trades can provide a meaningful and lucrative career.

We see through social media—and even local trends—a reinvention of old-fashioned activities and simple lifestyles.

Influencers are baking bread and sharing their experiences on social media. Kids are canning and making jam. People are leaving cities to explore agriculture and homesteading.

My grandfather Tim Ottink (back centre) learning mechanics in the Netherlands as a school boy.

People are learning welding, blacksmithing, and

woodworking through online courses. It's not that young people don't want to learn the trades of their parents and grandparents. They are learning them in different ways.

Ironically, social media has contributed to the rise in popularity of the trades. TikTok, in particular, has been a great platform for tradespeople to show off their experience and skills and gain tons of followers. Viral TikTok woodworkers have inspired thousands of new woodworkers with the butcherblock and live-edge trends of 2020 to 2023.

With a spotlight directed back on the trades through funding, advertising, social media, and even the wave of AI changing computer jobs, we're seeing a rise in interest in getting back into skilled-trades jobs. Young people are looking for meaningful, well-paying jobs that let them work away from a desk.

So now that we have caught the attention of young people, we need to create an environment that retains and trains them well.

Myth: Young People Don't Want Your Business

It's not unusual for a business owner to confide in one of our coaches that he's ready to retire, but he doesn't think his kids want to take over. As I've mentioned, thousands of profitable, well-established businesses have no one to take over. Their fate is likely that they will simply close up shop.

Here's the truth. What the next generation doesn't want when they consider buying or inheriting from their parents is the resistance to change and grip of control that the senior generation still has on the business. They want to be able to make updates such as switching to software platforms that will streamline operations and getting rid of the fax machine in the corner of the office. They want to make the workplace more pleasant for staff. They want to do things differently, and they don't necessarily want to buy your problems. They see how much you overwork yourself at great personal cost, and they don't want that for themselves.

The next generation of owners is eager to buy or inherit an established business when they see the potential, but only if they can have a clean transition without feeling like a little kid in the process.

They need help accessing the capital to purchase the business, and they need free rein to make changes that will sustain growth long-term.

I have seen young people set up competing businesses against their former employers and even against their family businesses. That makes for an awkward Christmas dinner. Sadly, it can be easier for a young person to set up something fresh, free of the emotional baggage and old filing cabinets filled with 20 years' worth of receipts.

Myth: The Trades Industry is Boring

The industry isn't dusty or dull. Yes, in many places it's still traditional—and sometimes outdated—but it's also absolutely ripe for innovation. There will always be hand tools and tried-and-true methods we won't abandon, especially where precision and craftsmanship matter most. But there's plenty of room to improve, and the market is already responding.

Tools are being upgraded to be lighter, easier to grip, and

less punishing on the body—designed for a wider range of workers, including women.

Computerized machinery, robotics, and automation are also making real inroads across the skilled trades.

Construction tech is booming; new platforms help crews communicate, dispatch, check in on-site, and learn the job faster and more safely.

When you borrow proven ideas from other industries and apply them to the trades, the opportunities get exciting fast. You—and the young people you mentor—are in the best position to push that innovation forward.

This moment in time is very promising for trades. The work is real, the needs are clear, and the improvements are already showing up in the field.

Myth: Young People Don't Want to Work

When my company is helping our customers with their workforce challenges, this comes up a lot. We hear, "Young people don't want to work." And it stops there.

The truth is, it's not that they don't want to work. It's that they want more balance. They don't want to work overtime. They don't want to put in 60+ hours per week. This feels very challenging in an industry that is directly tied to the hours put in on a project.

Concrete doesn't wait for someone who needs to clock out at 4 p.m. Customers don't care that your staff wants Fridays off. Sub-trades need to be lined up with precision scheduling.

So, this is frustrating for trades leaders to deal with. And the reality is that for Gen Z, work isn't their top priority;

it's not even their second or third priority. Maybe they've actually achieved this "work-life balance" thing we've all been talking about for 30 years. They're living it. And it's hard to manage.

It can be frustrating when you are in the middle of a process, and you need everyone to stay on the job until the work is done.

It's not an easy one to solve. We'll need to work together as an industry, listen to young people, reassess how to get work done with people working more manageable hours more efficiently, and maybe we can work less, too.

Myth: Investing in People is Too Expensive

Oh, I love this one. Some leaders say they don't want to invest in training apprentices because they'll just leave for a competitor that offers a few dollars more per hour.

This isn't true. What *is* true is that high employee turnover is very expensive. Your goal—everyone's goal—should be to reduce turnover. But that doesn't mean the answer is to pull away from investing in people. The answer is the opposite.

I've experienced horror stories. When things aren't working out, I've seen a leader's knee-jerk reaction to fire people. *Right Andy? Yeah, you know who you are. You magically expect new staff to perform within two weeks. If not, you fire them. But unfairly, you've not given them any onboarding or training. That's a really dumb practice. You're at risk of a lawsuit, and it's costing you big money every year.*

Don't be like Andy. Reduce employee turnover costs and

retain good hires by investing in people properly. Turnover generally happens for a few reasons:

- There is no onboarding and training—invest in onboarding and training, and people will stay.
- Managers and supervisors aren't great—people leave managers over the company they work for, so invest in training your managers.
- Communication is poor—a lack of clarity drives people away. Invest in improving communication skills and tools.
- Pay or job security is lacking—don't be cheap, and try to provide predictable work, or you'll lose people.
- The work culture sucks—make it a safer, better place to work and, oh yeah, stop yelling at people!

Look at your entire employee experience and identify the places where people are leaving because they don't have the patience to put up with what, years ago, people ignored. Invest in people, and you'll retain great people.

Myth: There's Not Enough Labor

Almost true . . . but not quite. There are plenty of warm bodies looking for work. But there's not enough *skilled* labor.

The problem is that we need to compress the timeline that it takes to go from newbie to competent.

We need to continue attracting smart, hardworking, and interested people to the skilled trades. We need to provide lots of training. That means videos, hands-on mentors, and training daily and weekly. We need to document and film our work. We need to intentionally stack skills to train people faster, so they become useful sooner.

"Make room for people to fail without being failures," a training director told me. "If the trades can do that, we'll build real professionals, not just workers. Our industry's people challenges are very fixable. Better balance, better conditions, kinder leaders, more opportunities to learn and grow, and a sprinkling of hope."

Myth: Women Don't Belong in the Trades

Women have unique qualities that make them perfect for work in skilled trades: strength, stamina, attention to detail, delicate and careful work, emotional intelligence, and planning skills.

There isn't a lot that women can't or won't do in the workforce. It's not a question of "if" women can be in the trades; it's a question of making the pathways clear and known to everyone, women included. I'm happy to see companies, apprenticeship programs, and unions actively recruiting women.

Women entering the trades aren't asking for special treatment. They're asking for respect. Women raise the bar for the whole crew. As one veteran carpenter put it, "She didn't just fit in—she made us better."

The culture of the trades is shifting from exclusion to excellence, and everyone on site can feel the difference. I can't wait to see more of this. Seeing women rise to authority in the trades is a major opportunity to meet the skilled trades gap.

Myth: No One Wants to Hire Apprentices

This myth stings a bit. There is no single solution or easy answer to debunk this myth because there's an element of truth to the frustration. I have spoken to employers who aren't opposed to apprenticeships, but who do have reservations when it comes to taking on apprentices.

They are hesitant to wade in and navigate the weeds of paperwork and uncertainty often required to sponsor apprentices. Despite financial incentives from government programs, employers may have been burned in the past with red tape and heavy investment.

Employers are worried about investing in training someone only to have them leave once they start contributing as a productive member of the team. They want some assurance that apprentices will stay after graduating, which, of course, is impossible to guarantee. Apprentices will have a choice, and if a workplace isn't a great spot to be at, they will leave once they complete training. Employers also want those seeking apprenticeships to be assertive, show up in person, shake hands, and demonstrate their character and personality.

The only advice I have to leaders of companies and unions is: Make apprenticeship training clear, engaging, useful toward examinations, and make the company a place where they want to stay. We need to become workplaces where people are attracted to join and stay long after formal training ends.

CHAPTER 4

WE HAVE THE POWER

A DECADE GOES BY IN A SNAP.

Ten years from now, if we keep plodding along with our heads in the sand, we'll be in a really bad spot where many companies simply won't survive. A third of the workforce will have retired. Profitable companies will have closed without passing on their legacies. Apprenticeships won't have started or been completed. Companies will still be operating in the old ways and won't have heeded the wake-up call.

All of the Toms, Lizs, and Jerrys will have grabbed their toolbox for the last time and will be hitting the links, fishing, and heading toward well-earned rest. And with them, their knowledge will be gone, too. The faint echo of their "Don't do it that way! You'll cut your hand off!" will slowly fade away to nostalgia. Who is going to fix our mistakes and help us save money?

Since almost none of the companies I've encountered have had any formal system to document, film, or pass along their information, most of their know-how will be unavailable to the wave of new hires. All we'll have left of Tom, Liz, and Jerry will be memories and folklore. Training will still be ad hoc and clunky, taking far longer than it needs to get people to the skill level they need to succeed.

Companies that haven't prepared will lose their competitive advantage. Excellent people will leave companies struggling to compete. Only the cream will rise to the top and get the contracts.

Meanwhile, a new generation of workers—Gen Z and Alphas—will make up the workforce and won't have a tolerance for toxic sites or training by osmosis. They'll simply leave if they don't find meaning and career opportunities. Millennial and Gen X leaders will need to take the best from their boomer mentors and revitalize the industry with the great things that they've been waiting to implement.

When the culture of this industry doesn't change, young people will come and go, never staying long enough to gain any mastery. They'll burn out or quit, and owners will be left hanging.

If a company is floundering now, it'll be out of business before long.

That decade goes by in the blink of an eye. You wake up one morning, and your hair is grayer, you have a few more lines on your face, and your back aches more than usual.

This is a warning and a wake-up call: We can't keep doing things the same way and expect different results.

We're in the industry.

That means we get to be part of the solution.

A Healthy Industry in 10 Years

If we want a healthy trades industry, we need everyone to work together: government incentives, education systems, training providers, apprenticeship regulators, unions, and employers. Since the bottom line is work output to meet demand for services and produce output, and workers need employment, there are four interconnected areas that employers can focus on to win.

The Talent Flywheel

The talent flywheel was born of a need to help companies recognize where they are missing the mark and out of sync with providing what staff and crews want. Not surprisingly, when leaders and companies give employees the right thing, employees respond with hard work, energy, and loyalty. It's a mutually beneficial situation.

Leaders are at the heart—the hub—of the flywheel. Their decisions and daily behaviors will impact the success of every single aspect of what's needed for a company to be an irresistible employer. It's up to leaders to respond to the need.

1. Recruit The Best

Companies can recruit the best people when they can prove they are stable—a safe and secure option. Young people, especially, are going to ask the question: "Can I survive here?" Rising cost-of-living pressure means younger workers are less tolerant of instability than past generations. You will win if you can give them:

- competitive, predictable pay
- reliable hours and schedules

- physical safety and real safety leadership
- job security and steady workflow
- policies that protect people from burnout
- and evidence in the hiring process that you have your shit together and there's a future with them.

Word spreads fast, and people trust Reddit feeds. Today's job seekers will do their research. They will know through word of mouth if your company is unstable, chaotic, or great to work for. They want a job that feels less risky than the other people hiring. You need to show up with professionalism and be well-organized to attract the best.

2. Build Teams

Companies that thrive will build crews who work well together and have each other's backs through good and bad. If a company wants to build this solidarity, they have to offer staff and crews respect to gain respect and engagement back. It's tough to work in this industry, and younger workers will leave quickly due to poor treatment. The way you treat people is a better lever for retention than anything. It's not a "nice-to-have." If you want to get a team that works well together, offer:

- clear onboarding early on in the role
- respectful and well-trained supervisors
- clear expectations and fair accountability
- zero tolerance for harassment, bullying, or humiliation

- leaders who can give feedback without blowing things up
- an environment where mistakes are coached, and it's okay to speak up.

Workers want to answer "yes" to the question "Am I treated well?" It's the employer's job to make that happen. Early turnover, low morale, and poor reputation will be indications of a bad workplace culture.

3. Retain Great People

When you find good people, you want to keep them. I'll let you in on a secret for retaining Gen Zers and millennials. Offer them *growth*. They rank learning and development as a top reason to choose an employer, and they leave when they're not given enough opportunities for advancement. You'll have much higher retention if you provide staff with the following:

- a big vision for the company that shows they have room to grow
- clear pathways for career advancement from apprentice to journeyperson, supervisor, and leader
- real training to help them upskill fast (Don't make them figure it out and learn through osmosis.)
- access to mentorship from experienced workers
- exposure to new tools, technologies, and methods
- and a voice in the company to share their ideas.

This is where a lot of companies go wrong. They hire people, give them a paycheck, and think that's enough to keep them and gain loyalty. It's not the way young generations are wired. They'll "quiet quit" and eventually leave when they find some place better that offers these opportunities. Smart companies realize that expectations are different and they'll tackle that head-on instead of complaining and doing nothing.

4. Employer Brand

The companies that win all the awards for being the best workplaces have worked hard at building their employer brand. Earning this reputation means they've done the work and they've earned loyalty from their crews in return. They've turned their crews into fans and given them a sense of pride in the company and in their contribution to it. Here's what successful companies do to earn this trust:

- They actually give a shit about people.
- They give people work that matters. They don't just offer employment, they offer community, a family, a legacy.
- They demonstrate and inspire pride in work quality and standards.
- They provide purpose and a sense of belonging to something bigger than a job.
- They create opportunities to pass knowledge forward.
- They recognize contribution—not just output.

The Talent Flywheel

Fig. 2

When a company has values, lives by them, holds everyone to them, and leaders practice what they preach, employees become fans. They dedicate their life to the place and will become your best recruiters. Purpose and community don't replace pay, but they help keep great people longer once the basics are met.

If we respond, resist the urge to stay the same, and align with the upcoming generation's needs without compromising our standards and values, the trades will have a golden era. It will continue to be the backbone of the economy, and we won't go out of business. We are the ones who do the work that can't be done by AI and robots yet. We are the ones who work with our hands, change lives, and impact everything we live in and touch. We have the power.

We can save ourselves from skilled worker shortages.

We can work smarter and use the people we have more effectively.

We can keep making good wages.

We can keep the industry friendly and free from mean behavior.

We can keep a competitive advantage and run our business successfully until we decide our legacy is complete.

CHAPTER 5

A NEW TYPE OF MINDSET

SUCCESSFUL TRADESPEOPLE GOT WHERE THEY ARE TODAY by working hard.

They are tough, determined, resilient, and relentlessly self-sufficient. This mindset has gotten tradespeople through recessions. It has kept workers paid, families fed, and deadlines met.

Ironically, it's some of these exact traits that are holding us back.

With the massive changes coming in the next decade, we're going to need to add some new tools to our toolkits.

The industry is changing along with people. The workforce you're leading today doesn't respond to the same rules that built a strong reputation twenty years ago. It's clear from the Talent Flywheel that leaders are the thread woven throughout the success of a team and a business.

Changing your mindset around how people are managed, trained, and led isn't about becoming soft. It's about becoming open and staying relevant.

Mindset: "I need better people."

The next decade will reward leaders who invest in people as seriously as they invest in equipment. This does require a paradigm shift.

What if, instead of hanging onto a "they don't make 'em like they used to" attitude, we shift our viewpoint to "I'll help make the next ones even better." Can you see yourself as a builder of people?

If you've ever thought, "I just need better people," you aren't alone. The challenge is, are you willing to think differently about how people grow, learn, and lead? And will you invest in helping people become better?

Mindset: "I don't have time to develop people."

Businesses have been built on the backs of owners and leaders who work 80 to 100-hour workweeks. Trades companies have been built on stress, lack of sleep, and overworking. It's because every hour not spent on bidding for jobs, managing crews, and fixing problems feels like time wasted. It's a time-for-money type of business.

For tradies, coaching people, leading people, and allowing them to come to their own conclusions and realizations feels slow. It feels quicker just to tell and dictate.

But if you've never taken time to build systems that give you time back, capture knowledge, and share processes and procedures widely, you're never going to be able to extract yourself from the operations.

In fact, *not* taking this time is costing you time.

Being needed 24/7 isn't a badge of honor; it's a handcuff.

You're in this situation because you thought you didn't have time to invest in people.

I challenge you to rethink this belief. I want you to recognize that when you invest in people and systems, you're actually exponentially increasing your own freedom.

Leadership and workplace systems are the only way to grow while giving you the freedom to have a life outside of work (vacations, time for friends and family, relaxation).

Mindset: "We can't afford to invest in people."

Back to the almighty dollar again. You may believe that training—investing in software to improve communications between crew, sales, and office—is all overhead costs. For years, industries have been conditioned to view human resources and training as costs that hit the bottom line because they weren't seen as investments with a strong return on investment (ROI).

But the truth is, you're already paying for it.

I dealt with a business owner who, I'll admit it, was a jerk.

His turnover rate was 15 percent over eight months. He would hire guys and fire them within two weeks if he didn't think they were cutting it. He fired haphazardly, and people quit quickly.

The culture was poor, and he refused to invest in an HR person even though he had over 100 staff. He had zero onboarding process and no training. He expected everyone to walk through the door and start being productive immediately with zero support.

Since the average employee turnover cost is conservatively 25 percent of their annual wage, we can estimate that, at an $80,000 wage, with a turnover of fifteen people in eight months, he had already cost himself $300,000 in turnover costs. That's money down the drain, wasted on recruiting, hiring, managing, setting up with equipment, and then firing and starting again.

Other costs you're already incurring include rework, reputation loss, and absenteeism. But there is more. Hidden costs that drain thousands more dollars every month include disgruntled staff, unclear expectations, poor communication, and "quiet quitting."

You're already paying the bill. You just might not realize it yet. I'd challenge you to invest in doing it right. Treat people as what they are—business assets that appreciate.

Mindset: "Touchy-Feely HR Stuff Doesn't Belong In Trades."

Human resources and training can bring to mind an episode of *The Office*. Cue the HR stereotypes that make any tough guy scoff and say, "That shit's not for me."

All of this talk of culture, emotional intelligence, leadership, and communication can feel like a threat to your authority.

After all, you've built your leadership on grit, not kumbaya and group hugs. But now that there's a fight for top-skilled workers, what's the answer?

The truth is that respect, trust, and communication are the backbone. They're foundational structures. A supervisor who listens and treats people civilly will retain talent. A foreman who can de-escalate, cut out bullying, and eliminate peer pressure that encourages unsafe behavior will save lives. A crew that feels safe to speak up will prevent accidents and costly mistakes.

A great workplace culture isn't soft. It's not just about feelings. It's also about how everyone shows up when you're not in the room.

An emotionally in-control leader isn't weak. And he's able to get feedback and hear about the problems without taking personal offense.

I worked with a big, tough trades guy. Unfortunately, he had some issues of his own that would bite him in the butt eventually. We implemented an employee voice hotline because the staff interviews revealed that no one felt safe going to leadership. They didn't feel like they had a way to say what was wrong in the company. This new leader didn't want the hotline. He simply wasn't tough enough to hear the team's feedback. He made us shut down that hotline because of what it represented—a threat to his ego. And by shutting it down, he just reinforced to the staff that he doesn't care about what they need. We won't be surprised when more major staff issues come up in the future.

How to Shift Your Mindset

Change will not happen overnight, and it doesn't happen by doing a giant overhaul. It happens when you acknowledge that you are interested in improving and then give consistent attention to making a change. Take action.

The 1-3-1 Rule

For starters, decide that if someone comes to you with a problem, instead of immediately solving it for them, you implement the 1-3-1 rule.

1. Ask them to be clear on defining one issue.
2. Ask them to give you three options to solve the problem.
3. Have them tell you one best approach.

This mental trigger will get you to stop fixing other people's problems. Every time you coach instead of tell, you'll be reminding yourself that you aren't the only person who can solve problems.

Prove the Cost/Benefit of Training

I know how much cost matters to trades companies. Margins are thin. Remember those hidden costs I talked about? Let's make them visible.

If you can stomach it, sit down and track, over the course of a few weeks or a month, all of your cost leaks. Estimate every dollar lost to rework, turnover, mistakes, injuries, wasted time, or conflict. Then total it.

All of these leaky profit-margin drips can be reduced with training. Compare all of the waste and figure the savings into your training and onboarding investment.

Consider how much it would cost you if your most senior staff, either in the office or the field, walked away, won the lottery, or heaven forbid, passed away. What would that cost you in terms of lost knowledge and reputation? How much does it cost you when staff leave because of their bad manager?

Sitting down and doing the math works because you're not letting cognitive dissonance keep you blind. You're pulling your head out of the sand, actually looking at the leaks, adding them up, and getting a reality check.

If you can't measure it, you can't manage it.

Prove It Works or Doesn't Work

To change your mindset that soft skills like communication and leadership are mushy and unimportant, we have to collect evidence and prove that being a great communicator is actually strong and important. Prove it to yourself.

Here's how to test and get that proof for yourself: Pick one crew, one project, or one conflict. Practice listening and asking more questions before jumping in with your opinion. Notice the outcome. Do people perform and respond differently? Over time, do you see better performance in the field when you listen, ask questions, delegate effectively, and clarify expectations?

If the answer is no and you don't see an improvement, there may be a few things happening. One, you may need some practice with these skill sets. Two, something else is going wrong that you're not aware of.

If the answer is yes and you do see an improvement in

how people respond and perform, congratulations—you're seeing the impact of tactical leadership at work in real time.

If you made it through this chapter and you are still closed off to these ideas, you might not be interested in the tools I'm about to give you.

If you're unwilling to change and you're going to dig in your heels at my words, you might want to put the book down now because the next bit's going to hurt your ego. I'm going deep into tactics, breaking down how to bring the talent flywheel to life in a real way and take practical action to become an amazing leader in the middle of it all.

Changing your mindset isn't about rewriting your firmly developed beliefs overnight. That's not going to work. No, it's about proving to yourself that by making some small shifts, the new way works better than the old.

CHAPTER 6

TRADES LEADERSHIP 101

IT FEELS UNFAIR. I'VE NEVER EXPERIENCED ANOTHER industry where leaders are so woefully untrained. They go straight from the trade to leading people without any preparation or education to help ensure success. Most training only focuses on safety supervision to avoid disaster and legal headaches.

What about training leaders to reduce mistakes, rework, conflict, wasted time, wasted labor, and injury?

Every day, people are promoted to supervisor and management roles without any leadership training. People start or purchase trades businesses without any business acumen or training. This is wild to me! Learning to lead by trial and error is possible, but it takes a long time, and it is very stressful.

Plus, fuck-up-and-find-out tuition gets awfully expensive.

Even union leaders are elected to prominent positions, immediately navigating software and business practices that are completely foreign. It's extremely stressful and risky. Administrative staff bear the brunt of this lack of experience.

Leaders in trades rarely get the support or professional management training that they need.

Good news: I know from training tens of thousands of leaders that leadership skills absolutely can be taught and developed.

A lack of skills is not the same as a lack of willingness to learn.

I get it. You learn best when information is immediately useful and highly relevant to your current work. You're too busy to waste your time. And you can smell bullshit a mile away.

Here's your condensed business school in a nutshell.

Leadership Skill: Vision & Mission

One of the pillars of leadership is the business's vision and mission statements. If your trades business has you feeling like you're flying by the seat of your pants and reacting, it may be that you don't have a vision and mission written down.

Get out of reaction mode simply by figuring out where your business, union, or department is going. If you have no clear vision, your business will be a snowball that does its own thing, largely out of your control, picking up clients that aren't a good fit, hiring the wrong people without realizing it, and making decisions that don't make any sense.

You must set the tone.

You need a vision for where you want to take this ship, and a plan to get there. Your vision will help attract people, grow teams, and retain loyal people. You'll remember this as a key part of the talent flywheel.

You need to rally great people around a big vision and a shared mission that they can get behind over the long term.

Your business's vision has to be big enough to contain each employee's personal vision, or they'll go and do their own thing without you.

Assignment number one

Get clear about your vision for the business or the team, write it down, then spread the word. Make it visible to your employees and your customers.

Examples of weak vision statements are:

- To be the best company in our industry
- Be the biggest plumbing company in the country
- To have 50 staff and $25 million in revenue

These are not very descriptive, and they're not very exciting for employees to rally behind. Let's try again.

Examples of vision statements that focus on the future and what the business will become are:

- To keep communities running with craftsmanship that never cuts corners
- To grow a company that our kids will be proud to take over
- To build the unseen systems that make life work— and do it with care

Next is to add a mission statement. Your mission statement is what the company does, who it serves, and how it gets that done. It grounds the business in the present moment and helps everyone in the business make clear decisions.

If you haven't yet done so, write out your vision for the future and your mission that grounds everyone today.

Leadership Skill: Strategy

Assignment number two

I want you to sit with that vision and mission and decide how you're going to bring it to life. There are many paths you could take "to grow a company that our kids will be proud to take over." It's up to you to decide how you're going to accomplish that. I suggest you carve out a day when you can set your phone to silent and plan for the upcoming month, quarter, or year. Involve your leadership team if you've got others helping you.

You need to decide how big you want to grow, how many customers you want to have, and how you're going to attract those customers. Then you'll need to figure out how many people you need to hire to get that work done. Where are you going to get your materials and supplies? How much cash flow or payment terms will you need to get them? This will be different for everyone.

Decide how you are going to approach recruiting the right people—those who care and are going to fit into your workplace. The key is to develop a team that can help you achieve that future vision while serving the customers today with your services.

Finally, you need to decide who will lead and what training they need to do so. It's your job to assemble a capable team with strong leaders so they can grow the business.

Part of your strategy will involve systems, because

teams can't run effectively without them. When I say systems, I don't mean software. I mean processes and procedures for getting the job done. The systems you need include how you approach hiring, onboarding, training, communication, sales, admin, service delivery, customer service, and more.

I've heard some excuses for not having clear strategies. I've heard these lines so many times over the years, and they're not strategies; they're coping mechanisms.

- "We're keeping everyone busy, so we're doing fine."
- "We take work as it comes and figure it out as we go."
- And my special favorite: "We don't need to write things down; everyone knows how to do their job."

These are weak excuses for avoiding systems, because they take the ability to plan for the future away from the leader. Avoiding systems leaves success to fate, threatens to crush the business, and inevitably, keeps the business playing small. If you do happen to have more customers than you can manage, it gets chaotic without documented systems for training, hiring, and communication.

I worked with a specialty trades company that had been trucking along for years. Their co-founders had grown the company to about 35 employees, and they had a clear vision. They wanted to be known as a great place to work that has a good reputation in their community for the work they produce. Trouble was, projects were running behind, and a couple of people who had been taking a lot of sick days seemed to be throwing everything out of whack. There were some risky situations with health and safety, and an obvious lack of training and policies. The managing partner was frustrated because he'd been hearing rumblings that employees weren't as happy anymore. They were expressing irritation that things aren't running as smoothly as they used to. After having to fire a couple of managers, it felt like a lot of the supervision was coming back onto the employees' plates.

After assessing their staff situation, we helped map out some strategies with them to bring their business into compliance:

- building systems
- introducing software that kept things moving
- sorting out training and basic employee success metrics
- hiring the right people and keeping them motivated

The new, clearer strategy kept everyone moving in the same direction. Everything is clearer across the board. They have a roadmap, expectations are set, and everyone is working toward that inspiring vision again.

Leadership Skill: Investing in What Matters

Bringing strategy to life does require an investment. Recognizing where you are going to invest can be tricky. Margins are more challenging today than ever, thanks to taxes, rising labor costs, and costs of materials. Regulations require more from businesses to operate in compliance. The cost of equipment, tools, and supplies is higher than ever. You have to be really intentional about reinvesting profit back into the company so that you see a return on that investment.

I want you to focus on putting money in places that save time (create efficiency), reduce costs (save money), develop people (improve productivity), and find and keep the best talent (improve effort).

Reduce Leaky Cost Wasters

I was talking to a leader at a multi-million-dollar business recently. He described their process related to tracking time and paying staff. Within about 10 minutes, I calculated that we could immediately save them about 70 hours a month, just by changing one process.

Why hadn't they thought about it before? Because they'd always done it that way and it had always worked—meaning people always got their paycheck. They didn't even think of challenging the status quo, even though it would free up 70 hours for more valuable work.

There are going to be many places in your business where you can find efficiency. I guarantee it. But it's really hard to see the forest when you're in the middle of the trees. That's why companies ask us to take a look. We will find efficiency, whether you decide to make the changes or not.

Software upgrades, HR and training systems, communication tools, dispatching software, time tracking, forms, and approvals; there are many tools available in the market that can help you and the people you hire become more efficient.

Look at your business through a lens of efficiency.

1. Look for the biggest bottlenecks in the business. Take note of where things are lagging, taking time, or getting stuck.
2. Where are mistakes and rework happening?
3. Who is poorly trained and taking too long because they don't know what to do or can't do it according to the standard that is needed?
4. Poll employees. Ask where they think time, materials, and supplies are being wasted. Ask supervisors and management for their opinions.
5. Do a time audit on key members of the team to document how everyone is spending their time. Now do the same audit on yourself.

We always start here because time is the greatest asset and greatest cost to any business—for you and for every other person you send a paycheck to.

Speaking of paychecks, if you haven't heard, there are more efficient ways of moving money around in the 2020s. I've not seen an industry more notorious for mailing checks and stuffing envelopes than manufacturing and trades companies and unions. But I'll not dwell on this detail.

Bottom line: Your staff will not be offended if you help them free up inefficient work. When you help them free up the capacity to do higher-value work by getting rid of dumb steps in a process, delegating to someone with a lower pay rate, or automating with technology, you save money and energy.

I think for so long, we've been programmed to think that to be a valuable employee, you need to just show up and grind. Here's a typical example of a time audit and how it helps leaders make a change for good.

Mark runs a glazing company with about twenty employees. He bought the business many years ago from an owner who handled everything themselves. The problem is, Mark picked up the same habit and is still doing everything.

When we first met at a conference, he looked burned out. He told me, "I can't get ahead. I have a lot of things I want to do, but I'm too busy just trying to keep things going."

So, I challenged him to do a time audit. It's not the most fun task, but I convinced him that it would be worth it. For two weeks, Mark tracked everything he did in 30-minute increments. It wasn't fancy — just notes on his phone: meetings, phone calls, interruptions, jobsite visits, estimates, problem-solving, paperwork, customer check-ins, *everything*.

When we reviewed it together, a pattern jumped out. Here's how his time broke down in an average week:

- 10 hours chasing paperwork and time sheets.
- 6 hours tracking down suppliers or following up on delayed glass orders.
- 8 hours reviewing estimates or fixing quotes that could've been right the first time.
- 10 hours on sites handling issues that foremen could've solved.

- 3 hours on phone calls that didn't lead to decisions.
- 4 hours checking text messages about customer questions
- Only about 8 hours doing the strategic work he actually wanted to do, which was building new partnerships, training crew leads, and planning for growth.

That's when it hit him: he was spending 70 percent of his week fixing other people's problems instead of leading the business forward.

Together, we mapped out steps that would change everything for Mark:

1. Control the calendar.
   - Block off important chunks of time where he only works on the business. He's not answering calls, checking texts, and being distracted. He gets done what he needs to get done.
2. Get a system in place.
   - Invest in a tool where employees track their time, submit paperwork, and do digital job reports.
   - Appoint ownership of documenting important procedures so they can be the point of contact for questions instead of Mark.
3. Tighten communication.
   - His office manager now tracks orders and updates a live dashboard, so Mark doesn't need to call around.

4. Delegate properly and give decision-making authority.
    - We taught him our delegation framework so he can stop rescuing his employees by taking things on himself.
    - He's learning to coach people after he's given decision-making authority, so they learn to think for themselves and solve the problems that they're responsible for.

A few months later, Mark said something that stuck with me:

"I used to think being busy meant I was valuable. Now I realize that being focused is what I should be getting paid for. I need to make those big decisions and leave the rest for other people in the business to handle."

After a couple of annoying weeks doing the time audit, Mark could *see* where his time was getting hijacked and where it would be better spent. He now has the capacity to recruit and train more workers, so he'll be growing his business faster than he was able to before.

Solve Employee Turnover Waste

I'm not talking about firing people. Not at all. And I'd never tell a home builder how to cut his materials costs. I wouldn't tell a hairdresser or a plumbing company owner how to cut their equipment costs. That's not my specialty. That's your specialty. I stay firmly in my lane—the people's side.

You can reduce costs by focusing on one important

number: your employee turnover cost. You can literally invest money and directly see an improvement in the employee turnover rate. It can cost anywhere from 20 to 250 percent of an employee's annual earnings when they quit or you fire them.

That's because you have a sunk cost that went into their recruitment: time to create and post the job, sort through applicants, interview, and hire.

You have the manager's time spent onboarding and training them. There are administration costs: training costs, equipment, software, tools, and more. It adds up fast.

Another client I worked with noticed staff were coming in and out of her business faster than she'd like. She had a turnover rate of 26 percent. That's quite high. We wanted to get her from losing eight people a year to three. The goal was to reduce her turnover rate to 12 percent, saving her $60,000 per year on this leaky money drain.

Hiring the right people and retaining them is one of my favorite ways to save money. Investing in a process to do this is a game-changer for cost savings. And it's measurable.

If you want to calculate your employee turnover rate and how much it is costing you each year, use the formula Employee Turnover Calculator.

Here's an example: You start a 12-month period with 100 employees, hire 35 in that same time period, and finish the year with 120 employees. The number of employee separations is 15, and the average headcount is 110. The employee turnover rate is approximately 14 percent.

Now, let's calculate how much this costs a company in a year. The Turnover Cost Multiplier is conservatively 60 percent of the average salary of $85,000. These are the costs for hiring, leading, training, recruiting, lost time, etc. The average cost to the company in these 12 months is $765,000. What could you do with that extra money if you reduced your turnover cost by even half that?

Employee Turnover Calculator

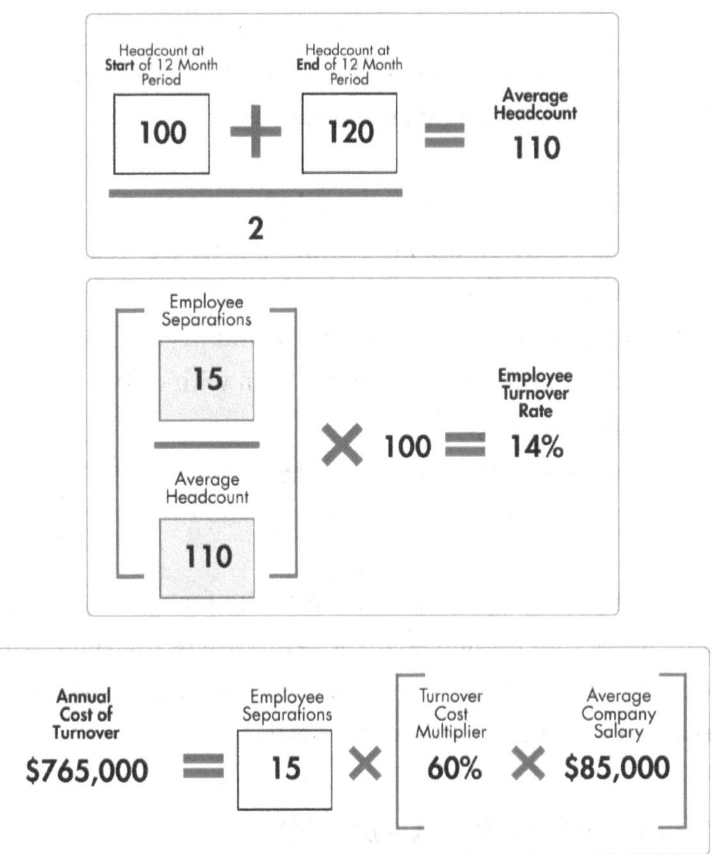

Fig. 3

You can use my online calculator by going to *www.boostld. com/employee-turnover-calculator* if you want a fast way to plug these numbers in and find out your company's employee turnover rate and how much it's costing you every year.

Some turnover is to be expected. And, if you have only two hires in a year and one leaves, you're going to have a high turnover rate, so use your head on this. But if you can see that the turnover rate is too high and you're losing good people, there are a few reasons why. (*Hint: it's not only because of pay.*) Remember the Talent Flywheel? I'll remind you again of the ways to reduce this wasteful cost:

- They may not like the workplace culture.
- They may be working under poorly trained managers and supervisors.
- They lack a sense of purpose and pride.
- You may not be providing them with onboarding and training.
- You may have fired them because they were the wrong fit or weren't who they said they were.

Fix any one or a combination of the factors above, and you'll move that employee turnover figure in the right direction. The thought of that can be overwhelming, so I like to break it down into manageable parts.

Leadership Skill: Delegation

A core leadership skill is delegation. You can't grow without a team that functions well. Your best key to growth and getting yourself out of the day-to-day headaches is to build a team that builds the business. Fine-tuning and flexing your delegation muscles is the best practice you can use to grow your business.

I've certainly learned this the hard way: "Hey Heather, can you handle this for me?" Heather is so sweet, likes to please, and doesn't want to be a bother, so she says, "Yep, I've got it." Two days later, I asked Heather about that thing, and it wasn't at all what I wanted. Feeling frustrated, I redo the thing myself. But now I have lost five hours of valuable time, rushed to get it done, and was late for dinner . . . again.

This frustration has very little to do with Heather and everything to do with the way I delegated the job.

Let's stop this vicious cycle. Next time this happens, and something's not working, get to the CORE of it. The CORE Model is a practical tool for leaders and supervisors. It helps to diagnose why a person, project, or team isn't performing as expected.

Here is a breakdown of CORE Delegation Framework

Clarity

Ask yourself: "Do they know what's expected of them?"

You can't chuck a job at a person and expect them to read your mind. Everyone needs to understand the direction, goal, and standard. Clarity comes from explaining what good looks like and checking for understanding. Without clarity, people guess. This guessing leads to conflict, mistakes, and frustration for both of you.

Ownership

Ask yourself: "Does the person have the skills and authority to own the outcome?"

When people believe the work is theirs to own, not someone else's problem, they have the confidence to move. They're motivated to act. Match responsibility to the person's skill level and help them upskill by showing them or teaching them if that's what is needed to do the job right. Remember to tell them that they're accountable by saying, "This is yours to run with, and I'm here for backup."

Resources

Ask yourself: "Do they have what they need to succeed?"

Check that the individual has the tools to do the job. They need enough time, the right support, and maybe even the people to do the job properly. When these things are missing, even the best people will get stuck. Before delegating and walking away, you can ask them, "What might get in your way?" and then clear those obstacles quickly together. The block might be red tape, budget, permissions, missing or broken equipment, or materials.

Energy

Ask yourself, "Do they want to do this, and does it matter to them?"

Energy is fueled by motivation, recognition, workplace relationships, a need to provide for themselves or their family, and a passion or drive. This is where you connect the work to the purpose or a bigger mission so they can get behind it. Address frustration and stress, as well as work overload. Too many years of overtime will end up in burnout. I'll summarize it: If you ask someone to do something, and it isn't done well, and you want to avoid these kinds of issues in the future, walk through each situation through the CORE lens:

Clarity: Do they know what's expected?

Ownership: Do they feel confident and accountable?

Resources: Do they have what they need?

Energy: Do they care enough to push through challenges?

Leadership Skill: Communication

At the end of the day, everything comes back to communication. Most misunderstandings and a lack of clarity arise from what is said and what is not.

That's why we invest so heavily in creating the best communication training out there. Our approach to training is very different. We make our students practice. There's no sitting passively in class or behind a screen dodging the hard stuff.

The prior violin teacher in me insists on putting every trainee, from top dog to first-year hire, through deliberate practice in real situations with a coach who can help fine-tune skills.

The hardest part about communication for leaders is that many people feel uncomfortable with conflict and say things that may be embarrassing. So, leaders shy away from the hard conversations. Or they're gruff and abrupt about it.

While it may not be something a trades owner necessarily feels they need, communication is the ultimate power move: being able to give feedback well, knowing the difference between telling and coaching, leading effective meetings, handling conflict, and more. The best leaders can handle communication with ease. Don't shy away from communication because you think it's a "soft skill." No way, it's the ultimate strength.

Leadership Skill: Giving GRIT Feedback

A powerful move for a leader is their ability to give feedback in a way that doesn't make someone feel like an idiot. You can give positive feedback freely at any time, but my suggestion is always to say more than "great job," which is lazy and not very helpful. It leaves the person wondering, "What did I do that was good?" and it makes it hard for that person to repeat the good parts of the job the next time. Be specific.

Equally, when you're giving feedback that's constructive and meant to correct or help someone do better next time, I suggest you try out our GRIT feedback model.

Here's how it would sound:

Ground it: "Hey, I noticed you walked off-site early yesterday."

Recall it. "That meant the electrical rough-in didn't get finished."

Impact. "It pushed the drywall crew back a day and created a shitstorm of messages."

Talk about the next move. "What happened? Let's figure it out so we can keep this from repeating."

Give feedback with GRIT and be nice about it (you're trying to empower people, not intimidate them). You'll notice things change around you. When your tone is calm rather than critical, employees will be more receptive.

Clear, kind feedback will create learning moments that build trust and improve performance. That's the real power of feedback: When done right, it builds people, not defensive walls.

Receiving Feedback

Feedback is both a tool and a gift, not just for you to give but also to receive. If you can deliver it to someone else, you should be willing to receive it from others. When you receive feedback, thank the person. Don't immediately assume that it won't apply to you. Think about it and then move on. Don't get your knickers in a knot about it.

Leadership Skill: Coaching

A leader wears many different hats. Sometimes you have to put on your "telling" hat. You have to give advice and corrections. Sometimes you put on your "training" hat. Other times, you have to put on your "coaching" hat. The difference with coaching is that instead of telling and giving advice, you ask questions and get the other person's input.

Coaching takes more time, but eventually it's the way to get someone to think for themselves and problem-solve on their own.

Coaching can happen informally on the spot or formally in a one-on-one meeting. It can happen in many different formats and locations. Coaching can happen at a coffee shop, in an office or shop, before or at the end of the day. Try to be present and ready to pay attention without distractions. We get the best success with leaders when we get them to schedule and make time for regular coaching conversations.

We recommend a very common framework for those formal coaching conversations called GROW:

Prepare for the conversation. Know what you want to talk about. Set the stage and tell the person what you want to talk about.

G: Ask for their Goals and what they want to work toward and accomplish. This helps you get to know what their career goals are, what they're working toward, and what they may be happy about or struggling with. The goal may be to address a particular problem or situation. You can talk about whatever you and they want to discuss.

R: Ask them to describe the current Reality. What would they say is happening now? Here's where you ask lots of questions. Don't start solving their problem or giving advice. Ask questions, then shut up and listen.

O: Ask them to give you some Options for how to handle the situation or get out of the problem they're in. Ask if they have ideas for how they want to achieve their goals. Get their input and get them to start thinking about how to solve their own problems and get what they want.

W: Agree on a Way forward. This is the commitment and accountability bit. Decide on what both of you are going to do. Commit to timelines and remember to follow up.

Coaching won't always happen in a formal conversation. You should also coach when you're stopping by a job or helping an employee figure out a problem in the moment. Rather than solving the problem for them, ask them to describe the situation, ask them for some suggestions that they have for how to fix the problem, and then get them to pick a way forward. You can ask them if there's anything you can do to help them or remove any obstacles in their way. But don't do it for them.

I couldn't hold the violin for my student and make the music. I had to coach my students to play for themselves. A hockey coach can't play the game for the hockey player. They have to help that player develop their own skills. We can't babysit or hold our employees' hands. But we can coach them to become confident to build the business under your values, vision, and with your strategy.

Leadership Skill: Deep Breath

If you have mastered some or all of the fixes in this chapter, you have already accomplished a lot. If you haven't, you may be worried you're fucking everything up. That's not the case. You're doing a lot of things right. And there are tons of ways to do even better, as you can see.

It's about creating a win-win situation for you and the people you lead. It's about making more money, getting more time, and not destroying your reputation in the process. If you want a strong legacy, you need to work on the whole package. This is the kind of work my team and I specialize in.

CHAPTER 7

WORKPLACE CULTURE

An expert on workplace culture for some of the most recognizable brands once told me that every company has a culture. If you don't intentionally create the culture, it will happen on its own. By leaving this up to chance, the culture probably won't be what you want. Whatever you have allowed, you will have to accept, because it takes a lot of work to fix a mess once it's happened.

I bet many of you within this first paragraph considered closing this chapter and moving on, thinking, "culture is stupid." If you did, this is probably the chapter you need to read most carefully. Culture isn't touchy-feely "HR crap." It's threaded through the entire Talent Flywheel and is the glue that keeps everything together. It's the tone and underlying message behind your success in recruiting great people. It's wrapped up in the teams you build and the way they treat each other and your customers. It's woven into the decision that apprentices and great workers make to stay or leave your employment, and it is broadcast straight out into the world through your reputation as a good or bad place to work.

We help companies with all kinds of cultural problems. I'll admit, the hardest thing to fix is culture. Once a culture goes sour or toxic, it can be very hard to turn things around. Why? Because the owner or leader who created the culture usually doesn't have enough self-awareness or willingness to realize they're the only one to fix it. They know the symptoms suck, but they don't want to change.

I'd argue that fixing culture is what could rescue the industry. Doesn't that mean it's the thing we need to actually work on first?

People are getting much pickier about where they work. Job seekers have career options. There are jobs today that didn't exist 25 years ago, and the jobs people will be working in the next 10 years haven't even been imagined yet. People can start businesses, freelance, become an influencer, or work remotely. We're offering tough conditions, noise, and dirt. To compete, we have to offer better.

Don't get me wrong. When I talk about workplace culture, I don't mean ping pong tables and energy snack bites in the lunchroom, as you might expect at Google and Apple. In fact, I'll argue that trades companies could have even better cultures and dynamics with crews than these tech companies.

The trades are made up of really solid people who do tough, beautiful, interesting work. There's camaraderie and teamwork, a vibe and a code among the crew; tradespeople show up and work together to get the job done. Companies and projects can operate like a family. It's a workplace where people have each other's backs and work like a real team.

That's culture.

Yet the industry has had a culture in the past that has been very unfriendly to many in today's workforce. We won't change young workers to suit an old culture that they think is outdated. The only way to adapt is for the industry to change to welcome Gen Z and Alpha workers.

I know, I know. I don't like it any more than you do. But we don't have a choice. If we want to stay relevant, we have to adapt.

Let's find ways to create fun and productive work environments that don't require cotton candy, pizza parties, and crochet circles at lunch. Let's talk about what works in our world.

Ingredients of Culture in the Trades

A good workplace in the trades has to have these ingredients:

1. Shared values and accountability
2. Trust and respect
3. Clarity and communication
4. Safety and well-being
5. Growth opportunities

If you leave out any of these ingredients, you're missing the mark.

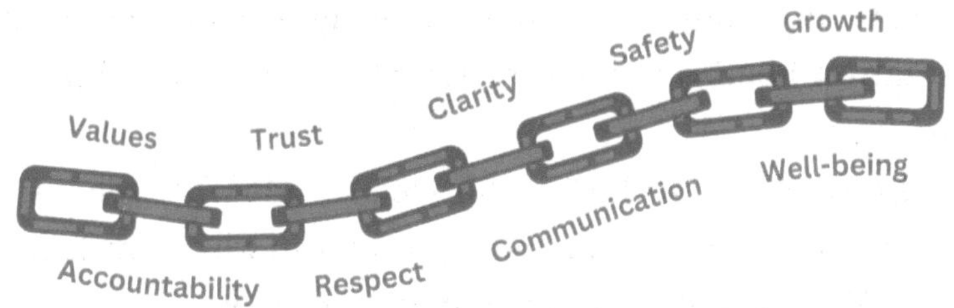

Fig. 4

When culture doesn't feel good, everyone knows it. We spend too much of our lives at work to want to show up in a place that's miserable, tense, uninspiring, and unmotivating. You don't want that for yourself, and neither do employees.

We do a lot of culture assessments as a first step for our clients. A lot of times, things have become so bad that leaders are at their wits' end.

The symptoms of poor culture are in-fighting, gossip, high employee turnover rate, disengaged people who don't give a shit, and toxicity. Tensions run high, company reputation is going down the toilet, sometimes there are lawsuits pending, formal complaints, or grievances, and nobody quite knows what to do about it. Leaders go silent and avoid conflict because they can't handle the tension.

What we discover at the root of the matter is typically insecurity, egos, poor communication, lack of clarity, and missing leadership. Occasionally, there are toxic people in the mix that have to go, but more often than not, we are looking at a combination of misunderstandings, hurt feelings, and leaders who allow bad behavior.

Poor culture happens when leadership does nothing to avoid confronting hard things or because they don't know what to do. Leaders need to have the guts to deal with the situation head-on, even if they're secretly intimidated and unsure.

Don't let this be the case for you. Decide what you want the culture to be. Be clear and write it down when you define your values. These values will continue to guide who you hire, the expectations you set, what you allow and don't allow, and all other decisions made by you, your leadership team, and employees.

There was a company we almost worked with that had a negative culture. On the surface, everyone was hired to provide a service, which sounded fine, but there was clearly a problem, because they had an 18 percent turnover rate.

Management was quick to fire anyone who didn't perform exactly as the owner wanted when they were hired. There was no onboarding or training. No evidence of values or expectations was communicated to employees.

The owner's go-to reaction was to yell. He had a temper. People were quitting for competitors who paid the same but treated them better. A division of the company unionized, hoping for better treatment.

While it looked like a profitable company on paper and was growing, this company wasn't fun, wasn't a nice place to work, and wasn't good for anyone mentally.

This owner didn't have enough awareness to let his leaders lead. He didn't establish company values and get out of the way. He himself treated people poorly and set a nasty tone for everyone. I don't think he is going to be around long-term.

Culture Starts at Hiring

A company's culture is living and breathing. It starts with the people you hire. A good culture is what attracts the right people in the first place. When you know what you're looking for, you'll weed out the wrong people who, although they have the skill, might not be the right culture-fit for the crew you're building.

When you broadcast your culture in the hiring stage, you will attract good-fit people. Show how you provide career pathways, how the onboarding process will work, what kind of training you do, and give smart job seekers a taste of what you're all about. This is your chance to give a realistic impression of what they're walking into.

Onboarding Sets the Tone

Once someone makes the decision to give you their 40-60 hours a week, you need to create a strong start for a new hire. Think back to a new job you had.

It can be fucking awkward when you start a new job. It's even more embarrassing when it feels like nobody knew you were supposed to show up. That first day on the job matters more than you know.

A great author, Mike Michaelowicz, said that when a person goes home to their loved one after the first day, and they're asked, "How was it?" you want their response to be, "Great, I'm really excited to be working here."

How can you create that kind of atmosphere on the first day?

Values, Principles, and Accountability

How do you create a culture that matches the values of the company? It comes back to values again. They are the backbone for a code of conduct that keeps everyone building in the same direction when you're not there watching. It's the written version of "how we do things around here." You might hold the value of Excellence, which you then operationalize through your guiding principles of "do it right or don't do it at all".

The guiding principles are the way that people behave to carry out your values. Here are some examples of guiding principles that crews can get behind:

1. Do it right, or don't do it at all.
2. Look out for your crew.
3. Make it right before you leave.
4. Own your work.
5. Teach what you know to save someone time.
6. Show up ready.
7. Treat the customer's home like your grandma lives there.

One of the best examples of culture done right comes from a unionized company I spoke to, which displays its values right on the wall. They start team meetings by recognizing people who've demonstrated values. The leadership team lives and leads by these words. They handle conflict amongst themselves, peers, and clients through the lens of their core values. And it works. The union members love working for this company.

When values are defined, visible, and lived every day from the top of the company down, culture is an advantage to attract the best-skilled labor on the market.

The beauty of values is that you can hold people accountable to them. You can say, "The way you left that job site isn't a reflection of our company value, *Excellence*. I need you to do it right." Or "The way you stormed away, leaving Dan up on that ladder, isn't a reflection of our principle, *Look out for your crew*".

People know what the standard is, and they know they will be held to it.

Do a value exercise for your own business and be honest. Does the place you lead live up to the values you *and* your workers want? Are people performing in a way that they're acting out the values and contributing to a culture that you feel good about? If not, get to work.

You need to be honest with yourself and only create values if you're going to stand by them, live them, and enforce them. Otherwise, it's a hollow practice, and you'll break down trust.

Trust and Respect

There are studies from every industry showing that companies that have a strong culture of trust and respect are more productive and make more money. There is also more innovation and learning in these companies, and they're more likely to adapt and be flexible to changes coming their way.

Having trust and respect in the team is a good thing.

Building trust isn't one-sided. It goes both ways and takes two to tango, so to speak.

Companies and leaders have to trust their employees, and employees need to trust that companies and leadership have their back.

When employees feel that they're trusted by management, they will feel a stronger sense of responsibility. They'll provide better customer service and be more productive. It turns out people are hard-wired to want to work hard in a place where they are trusted.

It's equally important for employees to be able to trust their leaders and the company they work for. Employees who trust what their leaders say and know that they will take action when there are problems are more engaged and work harder.

I have worked with a few companies in which clients' trust had been badly eroded. One of the obvious symptoms was that leaders were always away and unavailable to staff. Yet, somehow, they were micromanaging employees.

The staff themselves ended up finger-pointing, having a "cover your ass" mentality, gossiping, and were very guarded about communication. Quite frankly, people were not very productive, just getting the bare minimum done. They had some key people leaving because they were picking up all the slack and functioning despite the toxic culture.

Compare that to an environment where people are trusted: they work hard, they don't need a lot of oversight, and they certainly don't need minute-by-minute micromanagement. They can be trusted to handle customer needs and company resources. It's a more relaxed environment where people work hard because they want to.

That is what you want.

Respect is an interesting value because it's not just about avoiding being mean or openly rude. There are things people can do to be actively respectful—things like listening to other people and acknowledging that they're different from you and may have different skills or contributions. Respect is shown by giving people space to speak, especially when they disagree. Consider different generations. When you're listening to a person from a different generation and asking for their thoughts, it's respectful to actually hear them and not make fun of them or shut them down.

For a great workplace built on trust and respect, you have to focus on being a great human. The ego has to go.

If you've found yourself in a situation where trust is broken, it is possible to rebuild. It will take time, and you'll have to become a different leader to make it happen.

You'll need to welcome communication and be transparent. If people say something, you need to listen to it and do something about it. When employees see that feedback is taken seriously and turns into some sort of change, they start to trust again. It's tricky because once trust is broken, it does take some effort to rebuild.

Clarity and Communication

I will die on this hill. Communication is at the heart of all problems. To have a great culture, you need to communicate.

Don't assume people know your vision, mission, and values. Tell them and act them out.

Welcome feedback and give feedback that's meaningful.

Ask people for their input, and listen.

Be clear when you tell people what's expected of them.

Don't shy away from hard conversations. Avoiding addressing problems isn't helping anything. Avoiding conflict isn't healthy.

Create an open and welcoming environment for people to say what needs to be said and listen.

Hold people accountable for the kind of language you

expect on the job; if you have a culture of no swearing, address swearing. Yikes, I've already broken that rule in this book. If you have a no-bullying culture, call it out when you hear it. Whatever you allow will prevail.

Safety and Well-Being

If the term psychological safety makes you roll your eyes, you're not alone. The idea of having a workplace that supports mental health is absolutely not fully accepted in skilled trades and blue-collar jobs. We're recognizing how much this has to change—suicide rates have never been higher in our industry.

It isn't totally natural for those of us raised on "go out and play and don't come home unless something's broken or bleeding" to care about generations who need psychologically safe workplaces. We have no choice but to look it in the face and ask some questions of ourselves.

Let's start by defining it. What does psychological safety even mean?

A psychologically safe workplace is one in which it's acceptable for everyone to speak up, ask questions, admit mistakes, and share ideas without being made fun of or penalized.

If we don't make our workplaces in skilled trades and manufacturing psychologically safe, we'll die out.

We're in this troubling workforce situation because the industry didn't adapt fast enough to what the workforce was demanding. We're over here, jumping up and down, saying "pick me, pick me" to try to attract workers. Then we add, "But only if you're not a wuss."

It doesn't take much to create a safe business, not only physically but also mentally.

A place where someone can say they're struggling and get the help they need.

A place where mental health is taken seriously as a legitimate need and not brushed under the table.

A place where addictions aren't encouraged, but they're taken seriously.

I got involved with an amazing young operator when he had an employee who was self-medicating with recreational drugs and was killed on the job by a heavy-equipment accident. He and the owner were trying to pick up the pieces after this accident rocked his small business, and we were there to support him through the HR and legal consequences.

I have spoken to union guys who told me unbelievable stories of peer-pressured alcoholism and drug use on the job, and cases where new hires weren't trusted on the team unless they joined in on lunch hour binge drinking at a bar near the site. These guys are now advocating for changes in the workplace, but they're met with resistance from all angles.

What could it look like if anxiety, depression, anger, stress, and PTSD were recognized for what they were, and there were mechanisms to help through work? Better benefits, time off if needed, more openness, and less ridicule.

We would have a workplace that was healthy, enjoyable, rehabilitative, and welcoming for a generation that has more mental health struggles than previous generations.

Creating a psychologically safe environment starts from

the top, just like everything else. What leadership allows will trickle down into the entire workplace culture. Leaders can't allow ridicule, judgment, hate, and bullying.

Leaders have to set up mechanisms where people can speak up about problems, risks, and ideas without being shunned or burned. These crews will work faster and make fewer mistakes. A speak-up culture is a safety device and will save lives.

Culture Isn't Optional

If you're feeling called out in this chapter, it probably means that you know there is a culture problem that needs fixing. And, the good news is, it's repairable. It's hard to fix—but you're a fixer, right?

Culture may be the most important thing you work on improving this year. You decide how to reset the tone from the top down. Don't let ego get in the way of intentionally designing a workplace that's different from the way it's always been. Again, we've got to take the good from the past and let go of the things that aren't going to work for today and the workforce we're recruiting into the trades.

We've spent a lot of time talking about leadership and workplace culture. Next, we're getting into the heart of building those teams, retaining people through training, and capturing the knowledge from our top people before they head off into the sunset. Buckle up, buttercup! The next few chapters are going to be rich.

CHAPTER 8

LEAVING A LEGACY

On my optimistic days, I think boomers are the best. They're reliable, and they have so much practical knowledge. After all, my mom and dad are boomers, so I have an admiration for how smart they are and how hard they have worked their whole lives.

Then I have a chat with a group of boomers about their workplace and encounter the side of them that makes my jaw hit the floor. They're still putting a young kid on a broom and thinking he'll be happy there for two years.

Likewise, I spend time with Gen Z workers and can't help but think how curious, smart, and creative they are. I observe how open they are and how well they set boundaries. Then, I hear how much money they want to make and their expectations for career advancement in their first year, and how many hours they want to work each week, and I realize this generation has very different expectations from the ones before them.

The optimist in me will argue that there is always good to be taken from a person, a group, or a situation. The realist recognizes that we have to choose when to leave behind what isn't useful or good for us from all generations.

What We Take from Boomer and Gen X

What I will say about the oldest generations in today's workforce is that they have a depth of experience, work ethic, and principles that younger generations can really benefit from.

Boomers are in the final decade of their careers and are closer to retirement. They want to leave a legacy. They want to know they've had an impact and made a difference with their life spent in their trade.

They've worked hard, pinched their pennies, and are ready to hang up their hat and relax. They have put in the time (and the overtime), working in extreme conditions, and putting stress on their bodies. They've been underpaid, undervalued, and overworked. Many of this generation did so without much complaint.

We would benefit from embodying some of the boomers' best traits and values:

- Tradition
- Mastery
- Common sense
- Ability to tinker
- Love of family
- Willingness to sacrifice
- Loyalty
- Hands-on experiences and lessons learned
- Commitment

My uncle Ed Ottink passed away in 2025 at the age of 66.

Ed Ottink

He was a welder and general machinist and worked at the steel foundry Esco/Weir in our town for 45 years.

At his funeral, I was shocked to see a lineup down the aisle with men and women from his plant, all there with tears in their eyes, full of stories about Ed. They reminisced that he was the fun one, the strong one. He was the guy who never missed a day, even when he was injured or sick. He was the tough one who never complained.

He'd been retired for a couple of years at this point, yet the company lowered its flags to half-mast

Esco/Weir flags at half-mast.

in memory of Ed. That feels unheard of to me in this day and age.

When I asked my aunt about his time at Esco, she said he always spoke highly of them, and they had been good to their employees. It was a small town, and he probably could've made more money elsewhere, but when push came to shove, his loyalty kept him there.

It's important that if you want loyal employees who can live out their purpose, you have to offer them things like:

- a clear reason why the work matters (community and legacy)
- pride in craftsmanship and standards
- a sense of belonging to something bigger than a job
- opportunities to pass knowledge forward
- and recognition for contribution, not just output.

For boomers like Ed, the rules of success were simple (not to be confused with easy): work hard, save your money, give back to your coworkers, and remember who gave you a chance.

I recently spoke to a concrete company owner in his mid-50s. His biggest complaint about younger generations is that they have such strong boundaries on their time that they simply refuse to stay on a job until the work is done. They clock out at the end of their workday and have no interest in overtime. He said young workers don't prioritize their work. Work is simply there to fund their lifestyle. In his opinion, sometimes you need to stay a bit longer just to get the job done. They're not wrong. Sorry, Gen Z, we're going to have to find some middle ground to get the job done.

Another boomer glazing company owner told me that one of their company values is to tackle every challenge based on the Golden Rule: Do to others as you want them to do to you. The Golden Rule is posted visibly and literally dictates how leadership operates, and it is expected to trickle down to how staff operate. This is a company culture that is firmly rooted in traditional values and is very familiar to our older-generation workers.

We would all benefit from a sprinkling of these traditional values of "work hard" and "do to others what you want done to you" in our own lifestyles and approaches to work.

On the other hand, there are some things from the older generation that we can certainly leave behind:

- bias
- judgment
- peer pressure and bullying
- yelling on the job
- passing along the trauma of their workplace "upbringing"
- resistance to change
- and overworking and the hustle mentality.

There's always something good to take and some things we can leave in the past.

What We Take From Millennials and Gen Z

The under 40s. Those young bucks.

The millennials spearheaded a shift in the workplace that was very triggering to the establishment.

My suggestion when handling this generation is to be curious. There's equal opportunity to learn from millennials and Gen Z.

What makes Gen Xers and boomers such diligent workers is also what can make them feel frustrated and unhappy. They have fewer boundaries on their time and have prioritized work as their identity.

The younger generation has established that family, entertainment, hobbies, and enjoyment of life are more important to them than work. They may take it further than older generations are comfortable with, but there is something to be said for this way of thinking.

This generation believes that they can automate, leverage technology, work smarter and not harder, and attract people to buy into their solutions. They have a lot of confidence, and their assumptions are backed by technology.

Younger generations have so much good to offer and draw from:

- They're open and tolerant.
- They're innovative and receptive to new ideas.
- They think about how technology can solve a problem first, before anything else.
- They have high expectations for their lifestyle.
- They have great work-life integration and boundaries.
- They want better workplaces.
- They want to make more money.
- They want career growth.

I know young guys who are working four-day workweeks and are happier than ever. It drives their bosses nuts. But, instead of being annoyed, I suggest accommodating by staggering their teams so there is always client coverage. Gen Z and millennials are pushing businesses to think differently about how work gets done.

There are some things we need younger generations to reflect on and watch out for. Here are some traits that aren't so great:

- shortcuts and "good enough" mentality
- instant gratification
- lack of experience in tinkering
- less common sense
- distractable

Every generation has something great that we can all learn from and borrow. And every generation has traits that aren't good and need to be left behind.

Exit Strategy

This is one of those times where we have no choice but to play nice. Older generations will have to invite young people in. To leave a legacy, you need someone to carry on your work.

Older generations are worried that they won't be able to hand off or sell their businesses to younger generations because they won't be able to handle it or will burn it to the ground.

If you don't invite them to take over, the younger generation is likely to launch a competing business without you. And they'll likely be more profitable.

Their work may not be as good as yours . . . yet. But it will be.

If you're not careful to nurture them at the pace they want, they'll get in the trades, work for you to learn enough, launch a business, and figure it out as they go.

I've seen it happen.

And it will piss you off.

Startups will do it their own way, using technology to improve on the old ways that aren't working too well. They won't benefit from all of the good things and deep experience that older generations can pass on.

And that would be both a loss and a shame.

Let's Leave This Behind

There are some things we need to challenge the industry to leave behind.

Everyone in the skilled trades will argue that low bids kill quality.

To this day, when municipalities tender heritage repairs, the cheapest contractor almost always gets the job. Beautiful stone facades have been skim-coated with concrete, and ornate plaster replaced with drywall. Brick is being ground down to remove the paint. Exteriors are being repaired with wood that isn't suitable for the purpose. Today, the shortcuts that have been taken are calling in their dues and requiring repairs again from shoddy work.

A new generation of builders is refusing to play the low-bid game. They'd rather walk away from work than cut corners. Owners are choosing contractors who can explain not just the cost, but the craft behind their proposal. I dream that we end up with work that lasts, and clients who value the trades for what they save and the quality of their output, not just what they cost.

Leaving a Legacy

Some trades are doing an excellent job of passing the torch and learning from generations. Hairdressing and barbering are trades that not a single one of us would want to live without. This industry has done an amazing job of learning from each other, celebrating the creativity, excellence, and experience each generation brings.

I get excited when I'm on a jobsite with apprentices learning about old trades like stone restoration, or when I see young people learning about restoring heritage brick. I get excited when I see a new generation of carpenters restoring antique furniture or building windows and doors that fit seamlessly into a 200-year-old church.

All of the trades would benefit from closely observing how hairdressing, barbering, and other companies nurture knowledge and pass along experience while remaining open to ideas and modernization.

Trades are no longer a consolation prize for people who didn't go to college.

This generation isn't buying that story.

They see friends with student loan debt and no career. They see AI taking over knowledge-worker jobs.

They recognize that they can earn while they learn,

revitalize an industry ready for innovation, and have fun while doing it.

They actually do care about old ways of doing things, and they're proud of it.

CHAPTER 9

TRIBAL KNOWLEDGE

To be the company that is winning in the Talent Flywheel, the one that builds teams, retains people, and extracts loyalty, the one who is going to be able to pass the torch, you have to capture all the best from the people who work for you.

Your People Are a Goldmine

The kids are obsessed with "life hacks." YouTube and TikTok have loads of viral "hacks" accounts dedicated to sharing hacks for work, home, life, love, crafting, building, and more.

You and lots of people in your company have hacks too; you've just never formally written them down. In the working world, we call this tribal knowledge. Simply put, "The way that we do things around here."

The person or people with the hacks, know-how, or trade secrets are the tribal knowledge insiders.

Tribal knowledge is a collection of the shortcuts and ways of working that you and other staff have learned the hard way, which end up being your competitive advantage.

Tribal knowledge is all of the wisdom, stories, practices,

skills, and understanding that are passed along through word of mouth. This includes lessons learned on the job. It also includes custom ways of getting a job done faster and work-arounds when materials or tools fail, or you have to MacGyver something to work.

I recently captured a video of my dad in the workshop. He was building custom front doors to replace the ones on a 200-year-old church. He was really pleased with the chance to teach future carpenters a workaround on a basic piece of equipment, the router. He had thought through a unique millwork challenge and wanted it caught on video. Using a creative jig set up on his router table, he was able to run a straight edge, stick a pin through the entire jig, and finish routing on a radius. No doubt there's a robotic machine out there doing this, but for a small carpentry shop, these kinds of hacks and innovative problem-solving are the way things get done.

My dad, Neal Pope, in the shop.

Tribal knowledge is hard-earned, whether it's the perfect way to revive wood from a 200-year-old building, carve stone without it chipping, mix lime into a special stucco recipe, repair crumbling brickwork, mix a recipe of chemicals, or modify a tool to work just so.

Tribal knowledge comes from learning and trying. It comes from working through consequential mistakes that almost took you out—losses that you learned from and techniques you honed after years of experimenting.

Tribal knowledge is super important for the business's bottom line and also for workplace culture. Tribal knowledge:

- Makes everyone more efficient. You might find experienced workers come up with techniques to save time, improve safety, or use cheaper and more readily available materials.
- Becomes part of "how we do things around here," which can become a signature style, reputation, or competitive advantage.
- Shows that someone is a master with "tricks of the trade" that make him or her stand apart from beginners.
- Becomes an edge when recruiting or stealing staff from other companies, since people will want to work and gain experience at a place that is known for being great.

There are risks to having tribal knowledge left undocumented because when the information is not shared or written down, it disappears when people leave or retire.

Tribal knowledge, while being an advantage on one hand, can cause inconsistency because some crews or people may do things their own way, and quality can suffer. For example, if one crew has the know-how and a higher-quality finish but hasn't shared it with other crews, the company's reputation can suffer. Everyone will want that one "better" crew on their job.

When it's not clear why things must be done in a certain way, shortcuts or hacks can, in fact, be dangerous if novice people don't know why they're possibly hazardous. If a young person doesn't realize why something happens in a certain order, they may miss a critical step and get hurt in the process.

I think the biggest risk with tribal knowledge is when people don't want to share their insights with other people.

There are three risks with tribal knowledge that need to be called out:

1. **Loss of information.** When this information stays undocumented, we risk losing it over time.
2. **Impact on competitive advantage.** When shared formally with the right people in the business, it can become a company's competitive advantage, but it may also feel like giving away hard-earned expertise.
3. **Confidentiality and secrets.** Knowledge may feel confidential or actually be too secret to share. In this case, it may be a trade secret, which we will discuss shortly.

Often, tribal knowledge isn't formally approved, so the shortcuts and practices can feel like stretching the rules. Humans are hardwired to feel safe and protective. So, it can feel like it's safer to hold the cards close to our chest and not let anyone in on the secret sauce. But, how else will the next generation learn the little and big things that matter to your trade?

A training developer on my team who did a project for a major airline shared a story. Through training discovery, he found that the ground crew was operating outside of their procedures with a lot of tribal knowledge that was unwritten. Some of the "hacks" were great! And they got included in the new process that made up the training. But some things were identified as hazards through the training design process. The engineers were able to take a look at all the hacks and help clear up why some of them put materials on the plane at risk, increasing safety concerns. It's actually really good to see how people on the team shortcut, because you are going to learn something. Then, you can see if there is anything unsafe or incorrect about the other hacks and steer the ship away from danger.

I love this industry because almost everyone is a fixer, problem solver, and doer. Put a whole bunch of those types of people together, and you're bound to find shortcuts and improvements. The key is to get them written down in your business, so knowledge is better managed, captured formally, and shareable with everyone.

Tribal knowledge is like the seasoning on my best cast-iron grill. It's built up through years of use. It's priceless for sizzling that perfect steak. Ruined if scrubbed away and useless if no one ever gets to eat what I've prepared on it. It's meant to be shared. Ok, maybe I stretched that analogy a little too far.

A great process for you to capture tribal knowledge formally is to:

- **Document** the method, even if it's really informal at first.
- **Test** the "hack" to ensure it is safe, maintains high quality, and provides cost or time savings.
- **Refine** or approve the hack, treating it like a formal research and development project.
- **Integrate** the new method into training materials, procedure documents, and "how-to" videos.

Voila. You've created a formal hack that's just for your employees. "Your way" becomes a source of pride for staff. You can recruit people by promising that they'll learn from the best.

The Boss Knows Too Much

Maybe it's you who has all of the shortcuts.

Have you ever noticed that you get frustrated with staff or crew because they can't read your mind?

Do you get annoyed when others don't do things the same way you would do it, even though you know your way is better and faster?

I've got a novel idea: Instead of getting mad at them, write it down, film a video, make a checklist, or draw a picture of the steps, and teach it to everyone else!

What about another person on the team who has a tip or is known for a really good hack? Ask them to share it. Find out how they want to be recognized and rewarded for their innovation. Everyone likes to be compensated properly. You get to think of ways to encourage everyone to be innovative.

Pushback Against Sharing Tribal Knowledge

Let's remind ourselves that it was lame when Aunt Betty wouldn't share her prize-winning cake recipe with the other ladies at the auxiliary. Nobody is going to be hurt if that pineapple upside-down cake gets made by two people for the church potluck.

It may seem like it's better to keep your genius cards to yourself. It may seem like a lower risk of getting in trouble for bending the rules. Or you may think that if you share the information, you'll get more work piled on you. Or you may be worried that management won't do anything with the information or won't give you credit for sharing.

These are all valid concerns.

Real Questions:

- Do you really want to take all of the tricks and secrets with you when you're fed up with the place?
- Do you want to be forgotten and have all of your experience squandered?
- How many times have you been frustrated because someone isn't doing something right (because the way that you do it is the best way)?
- How many times have you stopped to teach them a better way?

Young people love hacks and want to know what you have to say. If you're not going to share your better way, Gen Zers are just going to get some weird hack from a bro on YouTube named "Handymanrizz." The cringe level is too painful to even think about, and the real good stuff that you're keeping under wraps will be forgotten.

Encouraging Tribal Knowledge Sharing

There may be genuine resistance to asking people to share. Let's dig into the possible excuses and pushback you might face so that you can plan to deal with them.

Tradespeople are generally proud of their work, and I think we can agree that boomers want to leave a legacy. You might try positioning it as: "Your way is the right way—let's make sure it's remembered." Ask people how they want to be recognized and how they want their legacy to live on. Maybe it's a series of videos that you pay them for, or a playbook with their name on it.

Treat people at the end of their career as the high-value person they are. Set up formal mentorship and training programs so when someone's knees are bad, and they're due for that replacement surgery, you ask them to be in a position where they're training the next generation, and they're being paid handsomely for it. Reward teachers, not just top producers. This is a mental shift that the industry needs to make.

We're going to talk more in the next chapter about how to train people based on the knowledge that's captured. At this stage, we're talking about sharing tidbits. It only needs to be quick and informal. Ask people to talk about their hacks. Get them to show and tell, then catch it on video when they're doing something that will benefit everyone.

Make two-way exchange mentorships. Novice workers can share their tips for digitization, software, using AI, and capturing processes on video, and senior mentors can share what they know with apprentices. I've heard from formal mentorship programs in the field that senior mentors end up learning as much as the mentees learned.

If all else fails, be direct. Say, "If your way saves time or avoids a mistake, that's worth more to the team than keeping it tucked away." Address the elephant in the room. Tell your senior workers that you don't want to lose 40 years of tricks and tips to retirement, and you want to make sure what they know gets passed on and not lost.

Share All The Best Information

I recently needed to get something fixed on my truck. When I took it to the dealer, they were just going to replace the entire part, which was a $1,200 job. My husband decided to shop around and found a mechanic shop that specialized in mufflers. The mechanic there asked if he wanted a straight pipe instead, because the flex pipe only lasts about six years. He offered to fix it for $200 with an off-market solution. We, of course, went for the better fix for the lower price. These kinds of shortcuts are only learned after years of experience. They're no good to anyone if kept secret.

Another interesting knowledge hack that I've noticed rarely makes it into training programs is using the sense of smell. Using the old sniffer isn't often formally written into training programs, but almost every trade uses their sense of smell in some way. Whether it's to identify a wood species, when you've run a machine too long, or to identify a source of fluid leak burning somewhere on a vehicle. These kinds of tips never make it into a college apprenticeship program. They're only ever learned on the job and are meant to be passed down.

Old timers have amazing techniques for cost savings and using what they have at their disposal. They're masterful at using tools to their advantage, the order in which to do things, measurement tips, and weather-related tips, such as how heat and cold impact metals, woods, and other materials. There are too many ideas to even list.

What have you learned from an old timer that's invaluable?

Here's how a trades business could begin formalizing its tribal knowledge without making it time-consuming:

- Dedicate a whiteboard in the shop for techs to add hacks and shortcuts.
- Have a 10-minute teaching portion of a day each week where you challenge yourself or others on the team to share something they've documented. After a year, you'll have a book of 52 documented company hacks.
- Have apprentices keep a digital log on their phones of what they've learned from their mentors. They can take photographs or videos with their phone.
- Create a visual checklist or procedure and post it near a piece of machinery or in a toolbox.

- Name the hack after someone: "Maria's manufacturing method" or "Pete's paint removal trick". It feels good and keeps that legacy going.

But . . . But . . . "We can't do that! Our ideas are way too secret to tell anyone in the company! We have to protect our knowledge!"

I knew this one was coming, and guess what?

I'm prepared for ya.

Trade Secrets

Truthfully, there may be some information that's too confidential or proprietary, and you're going to want to protect it from most of your employees, especially if your trade involves top-secret designs and missions like building the Mars Rover or underground bunkers for the global elites. Something like that you'd definitely want to keep under wraps.

I mean, if I were involved in top-secret spy detection radar development, I'd keep that information hidden from staff, too.

Trade secrets are classified as pieces of information that are valuable *because* they're secret. It's not really possible to legally protect trade secrets. The only way to protect the business is literally by keeping the information secret! Once the secret is out, the value is lost, and it's not something you can protect anymore.

If you do have trade secrets to protect, you'll know about it; I don't have to tell you what they are. However, for the sake of those of us who don't have such exciting lives, these are examples of trade secrets:

- Materials, chemical mixes, or formulas
- Manufacturing processes that are critical to your competitive edge
- Supplier or customer lists that may be rare or need to be kept private
- Unique tooling or customized machinery
- Specialized repair or maintenance procedures that make you unique

If you do have any of the above, and you know it would harm the business to let that information out, don't tell anyone. Zip those lips.

A pretty well-known trade secret leak was Tesla in 2020. One of their former employees was sued after allegedly stealing trade secrets involving manufacturing processes and data. Certainly, this is a big risk to companies when considering that employees may exit the company and go elsewhere.

You can protect yourself somewhat with NDAs (Non-Disclosure Agreements), by restricting access to facilities or keeping the information out of documents. I will warn you, though, that the best method to protect yourself from trade secret theft is to limit who has exposure or access to the information. Once it leaks, the cat's out of the bag.

Know the Difference

Let's be real, though—most of the knowledge that you're going to collect and document is tribal knowledge. This information is not proprietary, and it won't damage the company if it gets out to staff. It's the opposite. It will probably save the company time and money, make it more efficient, and cultivate better employees if it is shared. So, share away!

On the other hand, trade secrets would be very harmful to the organization if they got out, and those need to be kept private. You're not going to want to include any of that information in an employee training session.

Once you recognize the difference, it's easier to see how much can be shared without causing harm. Capturing knowledge is the most important thing we can be doing at this stage in our industry.

The way you go about capturing tribal knowledge can be as complex or as simple as you want. Knowledge capture can't be ignored because these human factors from our top people are the things that AI and robots can't compete with yet.

The next chapter is the meat and potatoes of how to get all this knowledge documented and saved for the future. It's a hefty one, but it's not a chapter to skip. Grab your beverage of choice and let's get into it.

CHAPTER 10

KNOWLEDGE CAPTURE ENGINE

*"If it's not written down, it doesn't exist.
At least not for the next person who needs it . . ."*

THIS IS TRADES TRAINING 101 ALL WRAPPED INTO ONE MEATY section, where I pull back the covers on my company's method of capturing knowledge and experience, sorting and organizing that information before delivering it as training to the next generation. I want to capture knowledge from the people who are experts in their field.

Knowledge Capture Engine

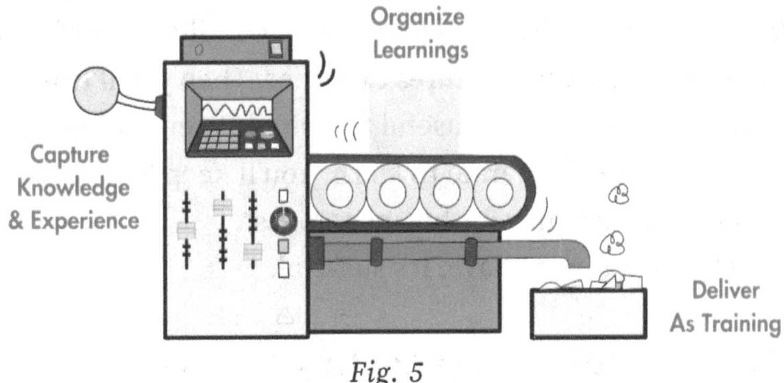

Fig. 5

Ready? Let's go.

Picture this: A master plasterer retires after 30 years at the company. He doesn't want a party, doesn't make a fuss. He just drops off his last timesheet, grabs his tool bucket, and walks out the door.

What's left behind? A few thank-yous, a text chain of inappropriate memes which will likely be the only thing that continues after he's gone, and a vacuum where decades of know-how used to be.

This is happening all over the trades. Unassuming exits with significant consequences.

We can no longer afford to treat knowledge transfer as an afterthought. It has to be intentional, structured, and embedded into the way we operate, just like compliance measures that you're forced to take.

Here's the hard truth: If it's not written, recorded, or passed down, it's not preserved. It is lost. And in the trades, what we're losing isn't just knowledge. We're losing technique, intuition, experience, and craft—all the things you can't Google.

I'll show you exactly how to turn that invisible wisdom, buried in corners and crevices of minds all over your company, into a visible asset. You'll learn how to build a knowledge transfer system that captures expertise. Then you'll learn to make it meaningful and useful for the next-generation workforce, who are desperate to learn. You'll keep loyal people engaged and set up your business to last.

This isn't nice to have. It's survival.

What Is a Knowledge Capture Engine

Knowledge capture is the process of identifying what's

important, documenting or filming the information, and organizing the information so it's useful to other people in the future through some sort of training. So, if your office manager is off sick, payments and payroll keep rolling without missing a beat. If your foreman is on vacation, you don't have to call off the job or jump in to cover because we have someone cross-trained.

Your Knowledge Capture Engine is the way to document your secret sauce so that when your top guy retires from his plaster job, others know how to concoct the perfect stucco mix for a historic house.

Others know the way of working that keeps your reputation strong and your phone ringing even in a recession.

This process starts by figuring out what is most important to document. Procedures, insights, methods, and craft. This could be everything, such as how to determine whether it's a repair or replacement, how to order materials, where components are stored, and instructions on actually doing the job your way. Of course, not everything gets documented; nobody cares about the toilet paper brand we buy. Focus on what's most important.

Then, we create a digital system to store and organize that information in a way that's useful for people. I know technology can sometimes feel overwhelming, but it doesn't have to be. Your apprentices and juniors are used to using technology, and it does not scare them. The knowledge capture engine translates what older people know into how young people want to learn. After that, we build a plan to keep the system updated and decide how your entire company will interact with it and learn from it.

Chances are you're already doing some of this, but it's probably disorganized. Think of it like a cluttered garage overflowing with generations of family items. Antiques, tools, mementos, old sports equipment, junk, and unidentifiable old objects. Everything's in there somewhere . . . but good luck finding it when you need it, and you don't even know if treasures are lurking.

Our job is to help you clean up that metaphorical garage—to sort through the mess, uncover the gold, and turn your hard-earned experience into a tool that actually drives your business forward.

Knowledge Worth Capturing

You don't want to bust your balls capturing everything. That's way too much work, and you don't have time for it. Let's start with the most important things first. What are the most important categories to document? Think of this as making your piles for the garage (antiques, sporting equipment, family photos, journals, tools, etc.) Don't worry about the golf clubs from 1923. They're not helping your game. But that weird piece of art? Now that might be worth looking up on an art auction site. In your business, the categories worth documenting could be any of the following:

- recipes
- pricing
- chemistry
- processes
- workflows

- best practices
- methods
- workarounds
- lessons learned from a project or job
- trade secrets
- stories
- case studies
- innovative ideas
- research
- historical (archival) content

Hold up. This isn't just for a few people at the company. Nope, it's for everyone. All of the jobs are important. Look at everyone in the organization as having knowledge that is important enough to capture for future use: leadership, managers, supervisors, project managers, estimators, and administrators. You don't want to be left hanging when the administrator is called away suddenly, one of the guys is out with a bad back, or another of your favorite masons retires and goes back to the old country. Everyone has something important to capture and store as knowledge assets.

Capturing Knowledge Assets

Knowledge assets are the individual documents that you capture, catalog, and store for future use. This can be super simple or relatively complicated, depending on the size of your business, the role types, and the complexity of your work.

In your business, the knowledge assets could look like:

- documents that explain a process with tips and tricks
- a standard operating procedure (SOP) or checklist to avoid rework
- video of a computer screen demonstrating step-by-step how to use the software
- videos of workers on a job showing a close-up method or procedure with voice-over narration
- charts analyzing historical information
- workflows that save time, show approvals, or decision points
- calculations, formulas, and expert geometry
- cut sheets or shop drawings
- and contacts, individuals in your network, and suppliers.

When we find ways to cut red tape and navigate a political landscape, we get deals done. When we know the tools to use and how to operate them safely, it saves us money and improves productivity. When we learn lessons from years of doing the same thing really well, we create a vast repository of processes. All of these could be knowledge assets for your business.

Digital assets

Digital assets are those that we capture and store on a computer (or the cloud). We're appealing to a YouTube generation. Everyone learns from weirdos online. Why? Because *we're* not on the platform teaching what we know. But our digital assets become our own internal company YouTube channel. The end goal is to have your own digital library where anyone in the company can learn and extract information from your knowledge assets. Digital assets look like:

- videos
- scanned or typed documents
- spreadsheets
- images
- audio files
- and transcripts.

I think of Julia Child's cooking shows in which she taught the world how to butterfly a rack of lamb. Who does that anymore, other than maybe Martha Stewart? But if anyone was going to do it today, it would be a Gen Zer with too much time on their hands, probably having learned the method from a Julia Child video on YouTube. The woman lives on . . . through her digital assets.

Physical and Intangible Assets

These are the things that cannot be digitized as easily. They may include:

- your relationships and network (keep track of these names in a customer relationship management software)
- knowing the right events and parties to attend (you can keep a spreadsheet with rankings)

- understanding the right hands to shake
- marked-up drawings and secret recipes
- and artifacts that are meaningful to the company's history.

My brain goes to my dad's workshop, where he had life-sized geometric drawings of twisted staircases and matching samples of carved spiral handrails on his shop walls. He also had old hardware specimens that can't be purchased anywhere anymore. They could only be replicated by ironworkers and other craftsmen if the job called for it. These are harder to protect from loss, but that doesn't mean they can't be stored with care, cataloged, and organized so they're easy for others to find and work with. Don't let the answer to "What's this thing for?" get lost with only one person.

Why Invest In Knowledge Capture

Most people or companies haven't intentionally worked on capturing knowledge, hence the ceiling-high piles in the garage. Most people don't even know what their people know. They don't even know the value of the treasures buried behind the boxes of dusty binders. So, if you're one of those who has never invested in knowledge capture, I'm sorry to break it to you, but there's a shit ton of work ahead.

There's going to be a lot of work to do to capture information that your mind hasn't even fathomed it's about to lose. It's no surprise we're unprepared. One hundred years ago, we didn't have to worry about this so much. Kids and apprentices had little choice. Kids followed along in the family business and learned young. They were often just happy to work and earn a living. They took up leather crafting or wood carving. They weren't gunning to be YouTube stars, Lamborghini-driving influencers, or UGC creators (WTF is that even?).

Knowledge was passed through generations. Kids learned alongside their elders. They knit with Grandma. They canned and gardened with Mom. They fixed their bike and changed the oil with Dad. Word-of-mouth and side-by-side experience were how they learned. Since that's not the norm these days, we have no choice but to sit up and pay attention. We can use relatively cheap and powerful technology tools and meet our next generation where they're at—likely on ChatGPT and YouTube, finding answers using their phone.

Knowledge capture isn't "busywork." It is work worth doing. Invest in the time and resources.

I argue that there are two reasons why we want to capture knowledge:

1. We're being proactive, capturing knowledge to get an edge in the future.
2. We're deathly afraid of losing everything in an unforeseen event.

Whatever your reason is, you may be feeling a gut punch from this book. It's okay—by taking this on now, you're one of the companies that will thrive and be future-proof.

Build the system, then simply maintain it going forward.

Imagine a global engineering company facing six of its most senior engineers retiring within 6 to 24 months. My team and I recently encountered this challenge. They thought they would have access to these guys for life. Guess what? Once these guys retire, they're not picking up the phone every time someone has a question and needs to "pick their brain." Thankfully, this company had a smart leadership succession team. They were worried about losing the collective 250 years of experience, expertise, best practices, failures, successes, and insights that were bottled up in those six guys tighter than their boomer emotions.

Our job was to set up their Knowledge Capture Engine—go back in time with each person, capture insights through interviews and storytelling sessions, do a show-and-tell with old blueprints and project documents, and ask questions directly from staff to squeeze out methods, lessons learned, and insights. This was a manual process, and we were up against a timeline critical to their organization's success.

If you're a mid-level engineer or estimator, wouldn't you want to be able to draw from the knowledge of a guy who has built seventeen bridges? Trades school and engineering degrees can't possibly teach all of this. Wouldn't you want to pick the brain of the person who drilled the oil fields in Texas for decades longer than you've been alive? This company was being proactive. They captured knowledge to help them remain cutting-edge. They're leading with a younger leadership team. They're going into the future, taking the best of the past with them, all so they can remain at the top of their industry.

On the flip side, we can learn from the company that experienced a devastating loss of documentation through an accident. Many companies and offices are one flood, fire, or disaster away from losing everything. Filing cabinets of paperwork are rarely backed up digitally. Union halls with over 100 years of history are not protected from the elements. People pass away, leave the company, win the lottery, or take extended leave for health-related reasons. Do you think Branko thought about downloading insights from his brain before he retired? Nope, never even crossed his mind. In these cases, you've lost your chance, and there is no making up for lost time.

Remember, we want to take the best from our experienced generations. It's selfish, really. We want to use that insight to train our next generation of workers. We want and need any edge we can take in this economy.

What To Capture

Let's go role by role and brainstorm what you may find valuable to capture. Let this inspire you and get the juices flowing for why you'd want to spend time and effort on this.

Knowledge Capture from Owners and Leaders

These guys and gals arguably have most of the knowledge stored up in their heads. They make loads of decisions. They understand the criteria they use to make those decisions. They don't even know why; they just act. Dave is still running his window manufacturing shop, and he's 75. He makes most of the decisions. It's so second nature that he didn't know where to start capturing his own knowledge.

When someone like Dave wants to sell his business, my team and I get involved. We have to be intentional when we work with these guys. We want to understand their decision points and get to the heart of why they do things. We need to understand their vision. We ask them who they choose to hire and why. We document to understand the strategy that drives their decisions. When a potential buyer is doing their due diligence, they will want to know what he's done and why.

These guys can be tough nuts to crack. Picture getting your crusty neighbor to crack open wide and let you in on all the secrets to his perfect lawn. You're peeking out the window with your binoculars to figure that shit out. Experts hold their cards close.

We usually hit them where it hurts. Ask questions that trigger an expert's sense of doom: If you walked out the door and never came back, what would be left undone that no one else would be able to do? They can usually list what they do that no one else is responsible for. Getting to the trade secrets is a little harder. You may need to keep the proverbial whisky rolling during the interview—that's when we get to the good stuff! That's when we start extracting trade secrets, things that they do personally to be successful, and the ace card they're holding back from competitors.

Here's what we collect from experts and owners:

- decisions
- decision-making criteria
- key relationships, contacts, and networks (the people they call to get unstuck and make things happen)
- the "right" parties and events to attend
- trade secrets

- strategy
- their vision
- recruitment or hiring process (if it's not centralized)
- passwords, legal/operational codes
- and calendar activities and routines.

The result is an Expert Playbook—a tidy manual synthesized from the information we pulled tooth and nail. (Yeah, we get the boring stuff too.) We capture the routines of work that must get done. We make checklists and decision-making trees, get private information (such as passwords and contacts), ask for thought processes and decisions, and sometimes, secret knowledge that, if lost, would be gone forever. All of this is turned into the playbook, one that their successor could pick up and use immediately to keep things rolling without a hiccup.

Maintaining Privacy

Don't panic. We know your expertise is private and confidential (*eye roll*), and way cooler than everyone else's. We're not going to post it to the internet. We're not even posting it in the lunchroom. We put protection mechanisms in place when handling private information.

Sometimes it only requires password protection. Other times, printed materials are stored in vaults. Some insights might be best passed along verbally, through storytelling and special handshakes. In this case, we won't write it down, but you're going to identify a successor to whom you will start sharing your knowledge and insights, so they aren't stuck and lost with only you.

It's typical for business owners and leaders to be the worst roadblocks in the pursuit of passing the torch. "Lifers" are those who have been in a role for a long time, say "I'm not going anywhere" (and mean it), and thus, may get a little nervous if you start to document their work. It is seen as a threat.

I assure you, no one is spying. You aren't about to get sent packing. In fact, you are not alone. If the knowledge capture engine is running, everyone is documenting their knowledge.

Union Leaders surprise me the most. This is a role that has the potential to turn over every three or four years during election cycles, and yet, in the cases where we get involved, there is no plan to document and pass the torch–all the work and insights—to the next group of leaders.

I've had countless conversations with newly elected leaders. I've heard more than one say they sat down at their new desk on the first day of their job. The outgoing manager handed them the keys and said, "Good luck." They had very little understanding of what was required. There was no manual. They refer to this as "trial by fire" or "drinking from a firehose."

I remember talking to one gentleman—and I do mean gentleman. His name was Larry, and he was the cutest guy from Kansas. He had to be about 75 years old. He was one of the only people who kept that union local office running. He did everything old school, with pen and paper.

I asked him, "What happens if he has to get a knee replaced?"

It turns out I'm slightly psychic; he had scheduled surgery

for his second knee in two weeks. He was planning to take his computer home so that he could work from bed. There was no one else to do the work. Poor Larry.

What is the most common reason union locals want a way to transfer knowledge? They remember what it felt like sitting at that desk with no clue. They don't want the next person coming after them to experience the same confusion and frustration. They know better and want to do better to leave a positive reputation and legacy.

Gathering Knowledge from Managers

I'm lumping foremen, site supervisors, and other managers of people and work into the category of managers. They're very close to the work and workers. They deal with most day-to-day questions and pitfalls.

Some of their biggest complaints (mainly in the construction world) are "I am sick of babysitting."

My answer to them is, "Stop babysitting! Create resources to answer their questions."

I invite managers to think of their role more like a parent—there to pass a legacy on to an offspring, not just to monitor some child for the time being. Parents of small children are constantly reminding, cautioning, teaching, assisting, and demonstrating. And for what purpose? To minimize risk and avoid disasters. Parents and managers both want to avoid spills, injuries, cuts, broken limbs, and destruction of their property. So, what do parents do? They watch closely, share openly, caution repeatedly, and answer thousands of questions.

If we don't want to "babysit," we've got to think of ways to answer crew questions proactively. Put energy into training them on lessons that will minimize risk, improve productivity, and get the job done better.

How do you know what to capture for this role? Think about the things that you need to *tell* and *show*:

- commonly asked questions to avoid repeating yourself
- processes and workflows so people can help themselves
- infrequent activities where enough time would pass between tasks that someone could forget the details
- tasks with step-by-step details and actions so you can make a checklist or guide
- examples of how you or the company likes things done
- video of how to do things correctly, explain what and what not to do
- best practices, tips, and tricks
- and insights and cautions

You may not know exactly what to capture because you're a long way away from your apprenticeship days. Ask staff and crews what they want to know. Make the content from their requests.

Apprentices and junior staff will automatically grab their phones to look up answers. We want them to grab our playbook to access a source we control. We don't want to rely on

Google and ChatGPT to inform workers. You want to share how it should be done in your company.

It feels good when junior staff can look it up in your system rather than be under your thumb. It will free up your supervisor to do their job. Once they have access to find answers themselves, junior staff will feel great not having to pester. Nobody wants to admit that they don't know something, so they may muddle through without clarity.

Capturing Knowledge from Senior Tradespeople

I was a stripper in my teens, and I learned from the best in the business. Keep your eyes up here, mister—not that kind of stripper! I was the kind of stripper who wears a Tyvek suit for her 10-hour shift removing paint.

Branko teaching me a paint removal technique.

The point is, I learned how to restore painted wood components on heritage buildings alongside some amazingly talented men from "the old country." They loved that I was sensitive to the depth of paint. I didn't hack away until I got to the old original wood below. I did a great job, and they knew it. They were happy to show me all the tricks of the trade. And again, it probably helped that I was the boss's daughter. I got to learn from the master himself.

That's really what we all want when we start out, right? Not to learn it from some bullshit textbook but to get it from the "old guys," the ones who've been there, done that, and have the "right" way to do it so it doesn't collapse, break, or need to be redone five minutes from now.

Senior tradespeople, craftspeople, and field staff are your gold mine of information. I'd argue we care most about capturing what they know. These are the craftspeople in your industry, the generations that know how to work hard. They sacrificed for their families to make money. They worked copious amounts of overtime. They dedicated their careers to one place as loyal employees. Today, they have aching backs and titanium joints. They're strong and staunch.

They hail from all around the world. They are the guys whose penmanship needs a translator. Their speaking may be heavily accented, but somehow they picked up only the most important words!

Capture the best from them. This is the torchbearer generation. Master doers and craftspeople. They put in their 10,000+ hours to master their trade or craft. Need a weird hack? Efficiency trick? Someone to say, "No, no, do it this way . . ." They're the ones who learned and taught themselves tips and tricks. They know how to jimmy rig a tool or reconfigure a part if it's not working. We've got a lot to learn. Let's capture their lessons, earned the hard way. I believe this is where we will gain the most valuable insights.

These guys take some work to get knowledge out of because they forget what it's like to be a beginner. What they do is so routine, like breathing, and they don't even know how cool it is. Who knew you could rub candle wax on a bit before drilling metal? Alex knew, that's who. Because his work comes second nature to him, his brain is running on auto. The job of a knowledge capturer is to interrupt that pattern and ask questions from a beginner's mindset. You will want to capture the answers to:

- How do they do something?
- What do they do to save time, money, and effort?
- What have they learned from someone along the way?
- Recall a project where things went really well.
- When was a time when they avoided disaster?
- When did they make their worst mistakes?
- What is the purpose of the weird tools and parts in their shop?
- What is their process, step by step?
- How do they make decisions?
- What do they wish young people knew about their work?
- What do they wish others around them in the job process knew about their work?

Warning: This is a manual process. You're not getting them to take this initiative on their own. You'll have to follow them around with a video camera and a microphone clipped to their chest. They may need to wear a camera and capture their point of view.

You might even need to convince them first.

You've got to record what they do and how they do it. You'll sit down with them to talk about historical jobs and ask them to tell stories about what happened. Ask where the project went wrong, what they wish they could have done differently, and why. It's your job to think like a beginner and ask the questions.

I'll warn you, it's kind of tedious. Do yourself a favor and hire someone to do the work to capture knowledge from this group of people.

Knowledge Capture from Operational Roles

When Raj, a senior estimator with decades of experience, retired, he left behind a binder of handwritten notes and markups—but no one knew how he always came in within two percent of actual costs. Another example of "Too late, bro!"

Construction professionals like project managers and estimators are another group of the workforce where you'll save a lot of money by avoiding mistakes and hiccups by capturing their lessons learned. They hold the budget and timelines. Even if your business isn't managing projects in the millions or billions of dollars, you still want to avoid loss. In this day and age, staying on budget matters. Profit margins matter.

Since these workers operate from software, spreadsheets, and blueprints, it is a little easier to capture their intelligence and insights. Technology can make the job of capturing knowledge easier. We use screen capture tools and software. These tools easily record a computer screen, which you can narrate. We have staff screen record their work all the time!

What should you capture from this audience:

- negotiation strategies
- how to get unstuck
- communication strategies to keep things moving
- thought process behind their work
- calculations
- data that goes into making decisions: ask questions like, "How do you know it's going to take three weeks to do that?" And "Why do you leave that kind of a buffer time in the process?"
- experiences: ask questions like "Where do you find the projects always start to waver and can end up with delays?"

Don't skip the people who work around this person. Raj may not even know what's unique about his work. But the foreman may have questions. The site supervisor will have questions. Project managers will have an opinion. Ask questions that mirror what others want to know. We want to know from management what they most want to know, so we can ask more intelligent questions.

When we capture knowledge from this role, we keep the end in mind. Who will interact with this information? If they were to interact with the information like it was a Google search bar or a chatbot, what would they ask? Those are the answers we want to capture.

Knowledge Capture from Office Workers

Office workers are the glue that quietly (or not so quietly) holds scheduling, coordination, and project momentum together. Without them, it's death by a thousand tiny bottle-necks. When Janet, the project administrator, took a leave because her mother passed away unexpectedly, her leadership was worried. If Janet doesn't do her subcontractor and supplier follow-ups, the whole project stalls. You end up with delays, annoyed customers, missed orders, and unbooked inspections. This ripples throughout the whole company.

Receptionists, administrators, and office managers are knowledge keepers of different kinds of information. They keep much of the business running from an operational point of view. Without them, it's no bueno. Depending on the company size, these knowledge keepers' tentacles can run deep through every department. They invoice, do the banking, and collect payment from customers. Staff members and vendors rely on them to get paid. Most staff wouldn't have the first clue where to find the information that this team holds.

They handle the stuff that no one realizes matters. The best ones know the names of everyone's husbands, wives, kids, and pets. They know when everyone's birthdays are. They're one step away from becoming a double agent. They can be a cultural blessing or curse, depending on how they're valued and cared for. Let's treat office staff with the respect they deserve and learn from them. Trust me, you'll be happier.

We can capture a variety of valuable insights from office workers:

- processes
- checklists
- time-specific work and routines—annual, quarterly, monthly, weekly, and daily tasks
- projects
- event plans and details
- back office contact details for the company lawyer, accountant, insurance, and computer logins
- emergency details
- key contact information for every account
- employee details
- decision-making criteria
- communications
- and notes from meetings and phone calls.

The goal again is to create role-based playbooks for cross-training purposes, to cover leaves and vacations, and to back up valuable processes and routines in case someone wins the lottery. And since they see ALL, we can take it a step further.

A common fear and misstep from leadership is forgetting to ask administrators for their feedback. I know, shocking, right? Ask them what they've observed in the company, where they see hiccups in the field process, where they think things could be more efficient, and what lessons they have learned the hard way in the office. This is information that other staff can benefit from.

It may be a good thing when your office manager leaves after 35 years of employment because she wasn't willing to adapt to the times. Or it may be devastating because you've lost a lot of the history, culture, and ingrained standards of customer service. Those handwritten notes and freshly baked muffins are often overlooked, as are her entire filing system and plans for the annual company picnic. When we look for the good in everyone, we will find that there's so much to share. Putting our ego aside, we will welcome the wisdom that's available from staff in every department.

Methods for Capturing Knowledge

Let's summarize the methods we've recommended for capturing knowledge.

Professionally Gathered

Manual Methods		Technology Supported
• In person interview with blueprints or physical documents • Storytelling • Mentors • Conversations	• Audio recording • Video recording • AI tools	
• Journals • Notebooks • Paper with handwritten notes	• Screen Capture • Audio Journals • Digital Documents	

Done by You

Fig. 6

On the bottom of Figure 6, we suggest that you can get staff to capture the information using either technology or manual methods.

On the top of Figure 6, we suggest how a professional can help you and take on the job of orchestrating all of this information capture.

Hire Help to Capture Knowledge

It's a lot of work to tackle a project like this. I suggest you get help to capture the large amounts of historical knowledge in your organization before it's lost forever. We help experts pass the torch to their colleagues, leaders, and the next generation of workers every day. We set it up and help you with the ongoing knowledge capture that you'll expect your staff to keep doing long after we're gone.

I have found the best way to get the information is through one-on-one interviews. It's time-consuming and needs coordination. We do the work for our customers. They're super busy, and so are their people. Taking the time to tackle this project probably isn't on the very top of your list of how you want to spend your days. Plus, it takes skill.

You've got to put on your professional information extractor hat and think like a CIA interviewer, ghostwriter, journalist, or instructional designer. You're on a mission to gather and extract information from people, then put all the pieces together like magic, sorting the information into something usable.

Our method is to be well-prepared and intentionally ask rich questions during interviews. We do preliminary research, we review documents to understand the business, and we ask people what they want to know and prepare great questions. These sample questions are from different points of view as we prepare to capture knowledge from one role:

- If someone were to take over the role:
    - What do you do that no one notices but keeps everything running smoothly?
    - What tasks take up the most time that you've learned how to do more efficiently?
    - Are there any tools, templates, hacks, or processes you've developed or modified that others should be using?
- If someone is reporting to the role:
    - What do high performers on your team do differently from average ones?
    - What communication methods work best for keeping the team aligned and productive?
    - How do you handle mistakes or setbacks so they become learning moments?
- If someone is directly impacted by the role:
    - What misunderstandings do others often have about your role that cause delays or rework?
    - Can you describe a time when better coordination saved time or money?
- If they lead that role:
    - How do you help team members troubleshoot issues or grow their skills?

- ▫ What kinds of mistakes do new hires tend to make?
- ▫ How do you coach them through it?
- If they owned the company that relies on this person for productivity and risk reduction:
  - ▫ What risks do you see in how this role is currently done that the company should address?
  - ▫ What opportunities are we missing because we don't fully leverage your experience?
  - ▫ Where do you think the biggest time or money is wasted in our current process?
  - ▫ If you could automate or delegate one part of your job, what would it be and why?

Once we're prepared for the interview and ready to start extracting the information, we'll use a combination of human gathering supported by technology. Here are some of the ways we gain insights:

- in-person interviews with blueprints or physical documents
- storytelling sessions
- observing mentor conversations
- and facilitated round table discussions.

We've heard it can be intimidating having a space set up with cameras and audio recorders. It works best when we're discreet, and people forget they're being recorded. This makes it easier for them to open up. If we need to use pen and paper to take notes and stay off the record, we'll do that too.

Honestly, though, we're rarely going to sit with someone and extract information without digitally capturing it in some way. When we interview someone in person with blueprints or physical documents, we're going to scan or photograph those documents. We're going to video and audio capture what they're saying. We're going to use AI-powered transcribing tools to automatically take their speech and turn it into text. We may facilitate and observe a conversation or round table between staff members and workshop with them.

Manja working with a senior trainer to capture knowledge via body worn camera.

Here are some tools used when we extract content with higher technology methods:

- audio recording
- video recording
- AI tools: voice-to-text, other AI-powered software

Younger generations (your junior hires) do this naturally. For one client, I suggested a low-pressure way to engage apprentices and capture knowledge. We sent a couple of junior staff members out with a tripod and an iPhone to a job site and got them to record from their point of view. We were pleasantly surprised when some creative TikTok-style videos emerged from that exercise. Don't worry, we also wrote a social media policy for you to block the videos from going public!

Knowledge Capture When The Pros Leave

There's always going to be stuff that will be captured along the way, even after the project is done. It's a never-ending process. You can take the documents staff share and digitize or catalog them on their behalf. Ask them to copy their:

- journals
- calendars
- notebooks
- paper blueprints with handwritten notes
- and models, work samples, and prototypes.

Raj, our estimator, was happy to leave behind his binder with marked-up notes. But nobody knew how to interpret them and get to the heart of how he hit his budgets so precisely. In the case of my dad's business, we have his geometric drawings and carved samples of handrails. Could we easily reverse engineer that? Not so easily. We need to ask him now how he got to the end point before it's too late.

Capture Knowledge with Technology

Technology has made it so easy to capture knowledge. Almost everybody has a high-powered photo, video, and audio capture tool in their back pocket. And if they don't, you can supply simple equipment. We might need to upgrade Rod's flip phone . . . *Sorry, Rod!*

Your desk people will have lots of documents from word processing tools and spreadsheets. They can easily capture their screens using video recording software, screen record, and screen capture.

There are plenty of AI-powered software tools that capture information in an intelligent way. At Boost, we keep our ears to the ground because AI is moving so fast. We find the coolest tools to use and build for our clients.

Anyone sitting at a desk, like Raj, Rose, and Janet, is a prime candidate for capturing their own knowledge. With a coordinated effort, it is relatively easy for them to get the work done. Use your apprentices to help capture work done on the site. It may not come naturally at first, but down the road, it could be the tool that unlocks the next big client.

Organizing and Storing Knowledge

Once you've picked categories of information that you want

to capture and you've started to capture it, **it's time to decide how to organize and store that information**. And no, we're not going to cram it all back in that "garage." We're going to put it all away, nice and tidy, thank you very much. Think of it as creating the shelving and deciding on the bins and storage containers that you want to use to store the contents of your garage.

There are many places to store information and make it most usable for staff. We're going to dive deeper into that in a future chapter. Patience, grasshopper!

"First learn stand, then learn fly. Nature rule, Daniel-san, not mine." —Mr. Miyagi, Karate Kid

We start with guidelines for setting up the organizational system:

1. **File Folder Structure:** Decide how you're going to organize your files and info—then set up clear folders that everyone can follow.
2. **Organization Software:** Look at the technology you have and decide on a new technology or software to store information.
3. **Rules:** Make some rules around who will be setting up the system and maintaining it.
4. **Standards:** Decide what "good" looks like and work toward that.

Anytime you're organizing files in something simple like SharePoint or Google Drive, or in something more complex and sophisticated, you need to set a structure and put rules around it, or it will get messy. We're setting up a system with rules so that:

- New information is properly saved and easy to find.
- Scattered documents and files get pulled into one place.
- Everyone follows the same system for naming and storing files.
- The right people can access what they need, when they need it.
- Old or outdated info gets archived instead of cluttering up the system.

Guideline #1: File Folder Structure

We've got to make some containers so the knowledge has a place to go. Think file folders. Before getting distracted with software and technology, use sticky notes or pen and paper, and draw out what you want. You can organize information in whatever way makes sense for you. Here is an example of sample structures that we have used with clients:

Knowledge Hub
    By Role
        Apprentice
            Lessons Learned
            Procedures
            Methods

Foreman
       Lessons Learned
       Procedures
       Methods
   Estimator
       Lessons Learned
       Procedures
       Methods
By Task or Department
   Concrete Pouring
   Concrete Forming
By Project Type
   High-Rise Residential
   Infrastructure

Guideline #2: Organizational Software

Where and how do you want people to interact with the information? Do you already use SharePoint, Google Drive, or a specific software for your crews? Think about where it makes sense based on how people already access information.

Make It Work Long-Term

It will get messy and confusing before long unless you set some rules and standards. Who's setting up and maintaining the file organization system? Assign the project to one or two people to work on the project as a team. They'll be responsible for policing how it's used, keeping it tidy, and making sure it doesn't fall apart.

Guideline #3: Rules

Nobody likes rules until there are no rules, and then every-one's begging for them. We haven't had any mutinies or revolts from our clients with this list of rules, so I'll share them with you too:

- All folders are visible to everyone in the role.
- Sensitive folders will be password-protected or will have access restrictions.
- All files are saved to a central location.
- Think twice before creating a new folder.
- Keep the system organized and check it regularly.
- Provide feedback to each other if folders or files are getting untidy.
- If you're unsure of where to find a file or where to start a new folder, consult the user guide or ask someone.

One of our clients, no joke, had giant master folders with thousands of files called Old 1 and Old 2. And they wondered why they could never find anything . . . SMH (that means "shaking my head" for anyone reading over the age of 30).

Guideline #4: Standards

Herding cats is hard. But at least they don't name their files *FinalFinal_UseThisOne2.pdf*. You've gotta set standards for naming files and folders, or it will get crazy. We go so far as to control the way folders "nest" underneath each other, so you're not clicking around for days. Here are the rules we use:

Basic Rules for Naming Files

1. Use clear, descriptive names.
2. Avoid special characters (except underscores and hyphens).
3. Include relevant information such as date, project name, or version number.
4. Use a consistent format for dates: YYYY-MM-DD.

Examples of File Names

- For staff files:
  LastName_FirstName_####_FormName
  Example: Smith_John_1234_SafetyForm
- For vendor files:
  CompanyName_DocumentType_YYYY-MM-DD
  Example: ACME_ProjectRates_2025-07-17
- For general documents:
  DocumentType_Description_YYYY-MM-DD
  Example: Policy_FileName_2025-07-17

How to Keep Documents Private

Privacy is so important. But you don't want files and folders buried so deep that nobody can ever find them again. There's this nifty thing called password protection. Yeah . . . It's pretty awesome. Use it.

By default, all folders that are shared with everyone should be seen by everyone. For sensitive info, change the sharing settings so only the right people can access it. You can set up teams or departments and share files that way. And, for highly sensitive files, add a password for extra protection. If it's SUPER SUPER TOP SECRET, you can store it in a vault with your gold bars and dirty secrets.

Knowledge is Slipping Through Our Fingers— And It Doesn't Have To

Breathe In . . . Breathe Out . . . Knowledge capture is a process. Capturing historic knowledge can be tedious and time-consuming, but please, for the love of God, don't skip it! Don't lose hundreds of years of experience from your senior staff. Don't let innovations, research, trade secrets, and best practices disappear. Don't let your insights, knowledge, and practices get lost to history. Prioritize this work.

Pull everything out of the garage, sort it into categories, build the shelving and storage container, and put things back in order. It will make the next phase so much less chaotic. Let's call it what it is: a Knowledge Capture Engine. Not because we like fancy jargon, but because this is a machine built to save your business from losing its most valuable asset: its people's wisdom. Some of this information will turn into training, but not all of it. I'm going to show you how to take the stuff that's worthy of training and deal with that in the next chapter.

CHAPTER 11

PASS THE TORCH

ARE YOU OKAY? DO YOU NEED CHOCOLATE? A WORKOUT TO blow off some steam? Did you make it through the last chapter? If you're overwhelmed, that's normal.

It's a lot of work to capture knowledge from the people who work for you.

The goal of knowledge capture and transfer is to pass the torch, to take the warm bodies joining the trade and turn them into useful workers—people who give a shit about the work, have the skills to work, and who can become productive relatively quickly without relying on osmosis. We have to shorten their path to mastery or, at the very least, competence, as fast as possible if we're going to keep up.

The next big question in this process is: If we do all this work to capture knowledge, how do we make it useful as training? We didn't invest all that time to let things sit on a shelf or in a computer folder and never get passed along to other departments or down to new hires. It wasn't supposed to be a make-work project. No one has time for that shit.

Well, here's what you're *not* going to do: huddle the guys in the morning, bring donuts, and have a sharing circle. I mean, nothing wrong with donuts and a huddle, but we can do more.

Your Learning Ecosystem

Every company needs to think about training and knowledge transfer as an ecosystem, working together. Do you have a system that's helping people get better every day, or is it leaving them to figure out their job the hard way?

Remember, anyone with less than eight years of experience on the job needs training if they're going to get skilled fast enough to keep up with demand and replace those retirees.

Simply put, a learning ecosystem helps your people get access to the skill practice, content, and courses in an easy way using technology and trainers. The content is carefully designed based on your strategy for what each role needs to learn. The fact that you invest in training, you pay people to take courses, and you encourage them to continuously learn is the attitude that sets the tone for how training is respected.

When your learning ecosystem is strong, you reduce cost, reduce waste and errors, and retain people long term:

- New hires ramp up faster and make fewer costly mistakes.
- Experienced people pass on their expertise before they retire.
- Crews make better, safer decisions on the job without always calling the boss.
- Your company's way of doing things stays consistent across projects.

Voila! Your reputation is intact, and your bottom line is better.

The Elements of Your Learning Ecosystem

Fig. 7

Attitude is the way your company approaches and views learning. If your leadership (you or others in your company) won't invest in training, scoff at learning, or behave as if it doesn't matter, then nobody else is going to care. A positive attitude about training means you invest in learning, make it useful, keep it current, and pay people to learn. This sets the tone for how everything else works. Attitude trickles down to everything and will make or break the success of this whole effort. Are you finally convinced that it reduces waste and gives you a cutting edge? Language from bosses at the top matters.

The **Training Strategy** will include a budget for training and a plan for how much and how often people will be required to learn. It will set goals for each role in the company and outline what they will be trained on. It will guide all of your decisions.

Technology & Trainers is the way that training gets delivered. You'll invest in a technology that stores content and training, tracks and gives you reporting, holds onto certification, and helps you make decisions quickly about who has what training and can get on what job. Digital learning management systems (LMS) are meant to provide this container for training. Employees can see what training is available and what is mandatory. We have a spreadsheet that's 50 columns wide, which we use to help our clients pick the right software. There are loads of good ones, expensive ones, cheap ones, and useless ones on the market. Do your research, or ask me and steal our shortcuts.

People. At the heart of everything is your people. Our goal with a strong learning ecosystem is to center it around the people who work for you and need to learn. We always make profiles on who the learners are, what they need, and what will make the most sense for them to do their job better.

Doing things the old way has gotten us this far. If we want things to be even better and we want to recruit awesome people, we need to train them so they're really good at their job much more quickly than ever before. If we want them to stay with us through their entire career, a learning ecosystem is a core part of that next step.

Content & Courses. Some of the knowledge you captured will be turned into training.

There are a few ways to train people and pass along knowledge:

- Quick-access training resources
- Video, in-class, or virtual training
- Peer learning and mentorship
- AI chatbots

My goal is to show you some of the options that are working really well for other companies like yours and push you to think differently about what's possible. Let's look at how to make each of these categories practical for people.

Quick Access Training Resources

Sometimes people just need quick access to information. Examples are to-do lists, checklists, templates, and forms that are easily within grasp. Wherever possible, you don't want people to have to reinvent the wheel on a process; you want most things to be rinse-and-repeat. These are your practical, visible, hands-on supports that take any training you've done outside of people's memories and turn it into a useful, visible tool.

Here are some ways we suggest you tackle this way of transferring knowledge:

- **Jobsite binders or QR codes:** Every truck or job box should have a laminated quick reference guide or QR sticker linking to procedures and checklists in your information management system. You can stick them on vehicles, toolboxes, and clipboards. QR codes and binders are easy to make and super effective for quick access.

- **Checklists:** Examples include "daily truck inspection," "pre-pour concrete checklist," or "equipment lockout procedure." Anything that has a step-by-step sequence that shouldn't be missed gets a checklist. Again, this can be laminated, taped to a wall, or in a truck, and can also be digital. Here's a good place to incorporate trade secrets like "Peter's Power-sanding Procedure." Make these documents handy. Don't store it tucked in a drawer under the paint samples, where no one will ever find it again.

- **Cutting or purchase lists:** Keep lists available for jobs or procedures if materials have to be purchased, cut to size, or prepared in any way. If you do the same thing more than once, make a list for it.

- **Visual aids:** These include posters in the shop that show tool safety, wiring diagrams, or installation sequences. Whenever we're working in environments where phones can't be readily available, especially in manufacturing facilities, we like to use visual aids so they're right in people's eyeline and don't require a phone.

- **Pocket booklets:** These are compact guides with key company standards, PPE requirements, and phone numbers. I've made many booklets for my clients that were coil-bound and designed to fit in a standard pair of coveralls, wherever phones weren't allowed.

- **Offline resources:** Offline and physically printed backups are a good idea. You can make digital versions accessible offline on company tablets for when the signal drops on remote sites. Print versions should be on-site or visible if something is really important. Desk workers can print sequences and processes and tape them to their wall. Sometimes, nothing beats flipping a few pages and getting to the information quickly.

The whole point of on-the-job resources is to help workers make the right decisions quickly without needing to hunt down a manager or supervisor. It helps avoid mistakes by reinforcing the use of checklists and sequences. It is much quicker to grab an already prepared checklist than to sit down and think one up on the spot.

We saw a company's mistakes drop significantly when they got intentional about their standards and made checklists and written procedures for employees to follow. It takes the guesswork out of everything.

Video/In-Class/Virtual Training

You probably already have training for employees, although I usually see everyone focused on only providing the bare minimum required by law for health and safety. I hear this a lot: "Fine, what do we need to be compliant?"

This shouldn't be where training stops.

Now and over the next decade, people will need more training than before. Trades schools and colleges aren't setting people up with the depth of skill or knowledge they need to be successful.

It's your job to bridge the gap.

Training today has to include problem-solving, communication, leadership, delegation, and critical thinking. These "soft skills" are going to be even more crucial than ever before.

As technology, AI, and automation take their place in the trades, human-centered skills and hands-on technical abilities will be the areas where we can do better than the robots.

My tips for how to think through training:

- **Video courses and libraries:** Show employees how you want things done with video tutorials.
- **Onboarding:** Set up a digital onboarding experience. Have a checklist for a manager or supervisor to follow. Automate as many of the communications or emails as possible. Follow your own checklist so you don't forget anything. Cover your company's way of doing things—safety, setup, communication expectations, and standards. Here's where you start to drill down on the vision and values so people know the standards that will be held.
- **Skill-stacking plan:** Each role will have a defined set of skills needed to master. Make a training plan based on all of those skills and check them off for that person as you go. It's good for them to see what they're going to learn and for you to stay on track with training. Shorten a new person's training

by years with consistent daily effort based on this plan.

- **Daily huddles and toolbox talks as training refreshers:** Turn everyday huddles or start-of-day discussions into brief training opportunities. Pick something to feature, drill people, and get someone to demonstrate something. Use these times when everyone is together to talk about and show what matters most.

- **Cross-training days:** Have field staff or various roles in the office shadow other trades or departments for a portion of the day to understand how the company works together. It's good for people to see how the different parts of the company work, what matters to their role, and why we are asked to do certain things. It's really helpful when field staff know the impact of their work on the office, on sales, or estimating, and vice versa.

- **Certifications and upskilling:** Keep a running tracker of who's certified for what (e.g., aerial lift, confined space entry, etc.) and ensure expirations are flagged. This can all be managed in the learning management system (LMS).

- **Career training pathways:** Map the pathways for someone from day one of their career to retirement at your company. Know the end-to-end journey and write down what kind of training, certification, or experience someone needs to move up through the roles. This is what will retain people long term. It helps avoid the awkward conversation when your employee who has been on the job for four years wants to become the foreman already. Instead of saying no, you can say: Here's what it will take to get you there in a certain number of years.

- **Human skills training:** It's a mistake to discount human skills training like leadership, communication, conflict management, and supervision. These are the fundamental skills that will make your company tick and retain the best people. Sign staff up for courses to train your leaders and help people interact better together.

We see a huge difference in companies that invest in formal training: everything operates better, people work better together, and it's way more professional and productive. Clients are happier because standards are higher.

There are fewer mistakes, less rework, and fewer accidents and injuries.

Employees like their work, are confident doing it, and know where their career can take them in the company.

Peer Learning and Mentorship

Knowledge doesn't flow only from training and formal booklets and printouts.

As we've discussed, a lot of learning will happen through word of mouth and side-by-side demonstration. Every company has tons of chatting, correcting, demonstrating, and discussing. This happens peer-to-peer and from elder to junior. Generations might not always understand all the slang, but they do understand a demonstration. They do understand stories.

There are ways to formalize this storytelling-style training:

- **Mentorship:**
    - Pair each new hire or apprentice with a specific journeyperson and tell everyone what you expect them to do with the time.
    - Switch up the pairs, and don't limit doing this only to the early stages of their career. As someone levels up and gains experience, pair them with someone more senior.
    - Formalize sponsorships among women in the trades so they can learn from other women who have gone before them.
    - Mentors and mentees can both teach each other a lot in the right environment.
    - Some people will not want to do this at all. And it may be best not to force them. A mean mentor isn't pleasant.
- **Mentor recognition:** Make this an attractive program so you encourage willing and cooperative mentors to participate. Give time bonuses or acknowledgment to mentors who contribute to developing others, especially as you have senior people that you want others to really learn from. Make training their job for a while and pay them properly for it.
- **Lunchtime learning:** Bring crews together monthly

to share "shop hacks" or lessons learned on recent jobs. You can buy lunch and bring in someone to teach something. Manufacturers or suppliers can train or do demos on their products.

The worst cases are when you've got an unwilling mentor to a young person on the job, barely talking to them unless they're telling them what they're doing wrong. I have heard a lot of horror stories about mentorships with unwilling mentors. We want to avoid that!

I love to set up formal mentorship programs with some boundaries. Usually, you've got a set time period. There are some suggestions for how to spend their time. It's not a "Velcro buddy" who never leaves someone's side. It may be an afternoon or even an hour a week working together. You can suggest that the mentee capture any of these moments or exchanges through video or by getting notes and feeding them back into your information management system if it makes sense.

BoostAI Librarian

Artificial Intelligence (AI) is the next frontier for trades knowledge management, and I'm really excited about the possibilities and what we're already able to do. I've been developing lesson plans and training for 20 years. The one thing I've always wished for was a Google-type search engine layered on top of every bit of training and information in a company. My biggest frustration has always been how to help people find what information they're looking for.

Now that we have AI readily available and pretty inexpensive to set up and train, we can do exactly this! I'm a huge nerd at heart, so let me tell you about my first demo that got me so fired up about the potential of AI for knowledge management in the trades.

The vision I had when I designed my first demo for a client was to create a digital librarian and an assistant all rolled into one, something that could be loaded and taught based on the content of our information management system and manufacturers' manuals. I wanted everyone to interact with it through a search bar. The chatbot would spit back a response just by retrieving information from what I gave it, without making anything up. Thanks to some techy friends who are way smarter than I am, we designed this, and it's so practical.

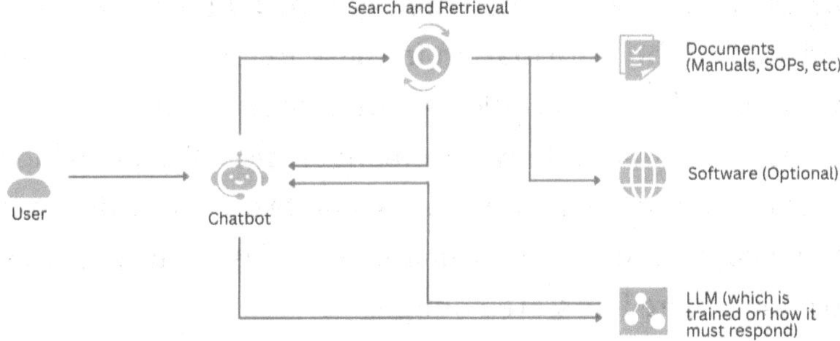

Fig. 8

Here's what the BoostAI Librarian looks like:

1. The user asks the chatbot a question.

2. The chatbot is trained by a Large Language Model (LLM) to answer in a certain way.
3. The search tool looks into every document it has been given and pulls information in the way it has been told.
4. The chatbot then replies with an answer from its search in all the documents it has been given and tells you where it got the information from.

I love this tool because we can be very strict with how it's allowed to respond. It doesn't get to make shit up. And it has to tell you where the information came from so you can fact-check it or get more context.

We had a client with about 45 employees for whom we built compliance training. All of their highly skilled maintenance technicians had to be able to reference about 40,000 pages of manuals and other documents to repair critical infrastructure. We trained the Boost AI Librarian to make sense of all the information in those manuals. The result was that technicians could ask the chatbot a question, and it would retrieve that owner's manual and tell them which page the answer is found on. It's a fantastic tool when you want people to access information really fast without having to know where it is stored online.

We're seeing small companies and really large companies invest in their own AI chatbots because it saves so much time that it makes sense, and the return on investment is worthwhile. Ask us if you want to explore designing this technology for yourself.

For training reasons, we're excited about how AI can be

connected to a learning management system to create personalized learning paths for every employee. The technology advances are getting more useful and exciting.

In this case, AI is acting as a buddy for our human workers, helping them access company knowledge and training in seconds without interrupting their workflow.

I know AI is a touchy subject for a lot of people. You, my friend, are in a sweet spot as a tradesperson; AI won't take your job anytime soon. It is more likely to become your own personal super-accelerant that takes care of the annoying shit that you don't like, leaving you free to do what you do best.

CHAPTER 12

SKILL DEVELOPMENT

EVERY CHILD HOCKEY PLAYER DREAMS OF BEING IN THE NHL. Some people make it; most won't. Many people end up learning to skate and play the game with some level of ability. Even being a pond hockey player requires some skill and practice to have fun. You probably couldn't skate backwards, let alone handle the puck, the first time you put on skates. It took a lot of practice, bruises, and patience to learn those skills.

Think back to when you first started in your trades career. Since I don't know you, I'll reminisce about my first time building. I didn't build a piece of furniture the first time I picked up a tool. I had to accumulate a lot of skills and knowledge before I built my dining room table. I remember the first time I used power cutting tools in the shop. It was intimidating. I was so worried I'd cut off a finger or maim myself. I was a violinist, remember, so losing a finger was a legitimately terrifying fear. For me to cut material to length on a chop saw, I had to learn some things—mainly, how to do it safely and how to measure and cut accurately. Every skill—from gluing lumber and using machines to sanding and finishing my table—was needed before I could put it all together in a piece of furniture that looked good and stayed together. Everyone has to start somewhere and build their skills bit by bit before they can do something amazing.

The most successful training in the trades incorporates skill development in a very intentional way.

We measure the success of training in four layers:

1. Did the participants like the training (smiley faces only please)?
2. Did the trainees learn anything? Can they remember it, and could they theoretically answer a test question?
3. Are they able to do something better as a result, such as use that tool, use the project management software properly, give feedback, or delegate properly as a manager? We want to be able to observe that someone is better at a skill.
4. Is the business getting a result from the training, either with less employee turnover, fewer mistakes, fewer accidents, or fewer injuries? Our goal is to cut the time it takes for someone to be useful on the job by 20-30 percent. If it would take three years to get someone productive, I want to help you get them there in two years.

How To Develop Skill

Lots of companies promise that their training develops skills, but it actually doesn't. Dumping more information on people in a 90-slide presentation will *never* develop skills.

The incoming workforce expects skill development; 86 percent of Gen Zers and 84 percent of millennials say mentorship and guidance are essential for developing skills. They spend time learning and working on skills. They know it is important, and they want skill development too.

The number one complaint in the industry is, "I can't find someone who knows what they're doing!" That indicates that we have a skill problem. Employers are looking for people with 10 years of experience under their belt and are having a hard time finding them. Since time isn't on our side in the industry, we need more people to gain skills much quicker so we can keep up with demand and make money faster.

The big question becomes: How do we develop skills quickly?

I wish there were a magic wand to make someone skilled in a super short period of time. But there isn't. My son is six. He is ready to learn an instrument, and when I asked him which one he preferred, he said, "Drums!"

I asked him why, and he told me, "Because I'm already good at that." He's probably traumatized by watching his sisters practice daily and go to weekly music lessons for years without becoming rock stars or YouTube sensations. I guess he's looking for a shortcut to mastery along with the rest of us.

I've been contributing to this issue of skill development since the very beginning of my professional career. A music teacher's main job is to develop skill, and eventually mastery, so it turns out we know a thing or two about helping someone on that journey. Here is my answer to all of the industries

I've worked in, especially those in the skilled trades: the key is deliberate practice.

Deliberate Practice

When you want training to stick, when you want someone to do something better and/or faster, you need deliberate practice. Not random practice—puttering for the sake of exploration, curiosity, having fun, or messing around. Deliberate practice is working intentionally to get better at one specific skill at a time. There are a few ways to set up deliberate practice for your own training.

Break Down Skills

One way to be deliberate about practice is to break down large tasks or skills into their mini skills. For example, there might be a procedure like skimming drywall. But let's break that down into four smaller skills:

1. Using the tools: trowel, skimmer, and hock
2. Mixing the drywall compound to the correct consistency
3. Creating corners and edges
4. Applying the compound smoothly

Each of these is a core skill that you can get someone to deliberately practice, so by the time they've mastered all four mini skills, they're competent at the main procedure.

It's the same thing for a musician. With my violin students,

I wouldn't just chuck a song at them and expect them to master the whole thing all at once. No, I'd break it down into practicing the rhythm component, then the tuning so the notes sounded right, then the bow technique, then the phrases and musical parts that bring the song to life. You don't try to perfect everything at the same time. That gets really discouraging for the student and sounds especially awful to the bystanders!

Recently, we built training to teach people how to use a device safely and accurately. This device had a time-based requirement that had a lot to do with safety. The training we built was distributed to tens of thousands of people, and we weren't able to teach the practical part to people ourselves. So, we made some digital components so everyone had checklists, videos, and images showing how to use the device correctly. That was the "show and tell" part. Since there was a major practice and speed component to using this device properly, we trained managers on how to practice this with their teams and assess each person's skills.

We broke the whole procedure down into the smallest parts for managers to practice with people. Our approach was for managers to do each step over and over until everyone could do it within a certain number of seconds. Their next lesson broke down another small skill until it could be done in a certain time frame.

It wasn't until the very end of the training that all of the skills came together. By the end of the practical part of the course, managers had to test to ensure all students could perform the entire procedure using the device within a certain time period. Any other way of training this procedure would have frustrated people. There would have been confusion, and there would have been a lot of fumbling, swearing, and walkouts. By breaking down the training in this way, everyone could successfully complete the time test.

I may be the biggest nerd around, but this jazzes me up. I love to think of something and break it right down so people can get better as fast as possible.

Focus Attention On Improvement

Another way to be deliberate about practice is to focus a learner's attention and effort on improving, honing in, and fine-tuning, rather than automatic repetition. The brain will always try to find shortcuts, and the brain is a master at automation. Deliberate practice requires someone to bring their attention to something and really work on improving that thing.

Let's say you're a hairdresser and you want to get really good at a new coloring technique. You'd decide to focus on practicing, take some time to slow right down, and practice something specific. For example, you'd put all your attention in that moment on changing the way you weave the comb through the hair, or tuck the foil, or something specific about the technique.

If you're a painter, you may choose to focus your attention on improving your technique when you're cutting in around trim. Simply putting your mind to the task and deciding to get better at it will heighten your attention and make you better at the skill.

When we create or conduct skill training, we find opportunities in a class to draw people's attention to something specific about the skill to interrupt the brain and get it focused. We don't want important details to get skimmed over or go unnoticed. For example, if you're teaching an apprentice how to accurately measure and cut a piece of wood, you're going to point out that the pencil marking is the actual measurement, and they shouldn't cut it off, or the piece will be short by the width of the saw blade. That's a detail that shouldn't be glossed over since it's important to the skill of cutting material to an accurate length. The student may be focused on other parts of the procedure, like keeping the lumber square, or not cutting off their hand! Arguably as important, I guess.

I'm obsessed with this one Instagram account of a Japanese master carpenter working with his student. In the last video, he was teaching the apprentice how to panel a wall with wood, and more specifically, how to identify which end of the wood is up and which is down, based on the knot pattern. He taught the student that when the knots are pointing in a downward slant, that's upside down because branches grow up and out. He spent an entire afternoon paneling a wall, making sure the apprentice stayed focused on which end of the wood was up and which end was down.

The same thing can be done on the job when you're helping someone get better at a skill. Draw their attention to something that may easily get overlooked. Or, say, today we're going to focus on improving our skills with this one type of technique. Get the reps in deliberately.

Work With a Professional

It's no good when you have the blind leading the blind. Someone who is mediocre or new won't help someone develop skills. Trust me, it never helps the situation.

When you have an expert or professional help develop mastery, that's when you'll improve fast. They can spot what you can't see. They can unlock that next level way faster than if you were doing the thing on your own.

A hockey coach at a bootcamp is going to spot the player's weakness, quirk, or body movement and can help correct that—unlocking a next level for the player. A music teacher can spot the finger movement that's limiting the musician. A golf pro can immediately spot why you're shanking the ball on your drive. They can offer a tweak that can improve precision.

When we design training, we want to get insights from the best and most experienced, as well as come at the concept from a beginner's mindset, too. We spend time learning from the best. We ask questions like beginners, so they don't skip the stuff that's easy for them now that they are masters. We want to know what the pros are looking for.

In the case of communication practice, I've had a lot of success with roleplay in almost every industry. Pairing a professional communicator who is trained on what to spot, how to correct someone, and how to play a character is the key to rapid communication skill improvement. I've even participated in this training, so I can see how it feels.

Practicing a skill like giving feedback can be tough. We're not used to giving feedback in a way that's well received. Our bosses just told us, "Don't do that." They didn't praise us when we were doing something well; they just told us when we did something wrong. You get to change that. Since we're not used to giving feedback that's specific to the behavior and explains its impact on the situation, we have to practice it.

Another example of a tough conversation is when we need to diffuse conflict. This can be tough to master because if it goes wrong in real life, the consequences are bigger. Practicing this skill with a coach through roleplay is great because the coach can tell you what you did wrong, and you can fix it in real time without anyone punching you in the face, crying, or calling HR.

We love incorporating communication roleplay into all of our trades training, from apprentices to leadership, because it's the fastest way to train the most important human skill of all time: talking to people. Taking theory and putting it into practice offers our clients the biggest bang for their buck every time.

When It's Safe To Try

The other thing that's important when you're upskilling through deliberate practice is to make sure the student feels safe to try. It's no good if someone makes a mistake and they feel stupid or if they're worried about getting in trouble. Deliberate practice is dead in the water if it's not happening in a supportive learning environment. Full stop.

What does this mean, and how do we set up a safe practice environment?

- **Set up practice opportunities where the stakes are really low.** Don't have someone practice on the most expensive material. Have practice materials handy for people to work on techniques.
- **Provide opportunities to practice outside production time.** Have some intentional practice lab time set up to teach and work on skills.
- **Communicate that it's okay to try, not get it right, and try again.** Nothing bad will happen in a learning environment.
- **Create moments after procedures to debrief.** Get the trainee to think—what did they do well, and what do they want to improve?
- **Stay open as a trainer to different approaches.** Beginners have a completely fresh view, and they're good at challenging the status quo. This is a good thing because they may have a novel approach. Efficiency and innovation come out of practice and tinkering.
- **Listen up and be open to ideas and input.**
- **Leaders should model a learning mindset.** They should show when they're figuring something out. This shows an openness and culture of a growth mindset.

Here's what not to do:

- yell at people
- make them feel stupid
- laugh at them

- shut them down
- allow employees to do this to each other
- and punish trying.

In our communications training, we seldom require role-play with managers or peers. It's awkward as fuck, and nobody feels "safe" doing it that way. We always include private one-on-one practice with a coach because when it comes to skill development, we want to be learning in an environment that's not stressful or nerve-racking.

Yes, the brain will learn when it's scared—it's a survival mechanism. If you almost fall off a roof, your brain quickly remembers ways to keep itself safe the next time. Neuroscience says that learning complex skills is tricky when the brain is in a high-stress situation because fear hinders decision-making and problem-solving. Turns out, yelling at people doesn't help them develop skills any better or faster. In an industry known for badgering people, we've got to stop doing that if we want to solve our skilled labor shortage.

Key to Skill Development Success

The apprenticeship programs we design have a majority of the time spent in the shop working on tools and technical skills.

It's not just tool-based skills that need to be practiced. People skills are equally important, and they need to be practiced too, including delegation, supervision, feedback, communication, and conflict management. Some of the best returns on investment for our clients are from these courses. People stay because of the good culture and good managers. The best way to create a great culture and great leaders is with human-skills training, such as communication.

We had one company that increased its leadership communication skills by 35 percent across several training sessions. We could measure that people were performing better when talking with trainees, and that means happier employees.

We had another company see improvement in their safety score. Their goal was to increase near-miss incident reporting. They knew hazards and incidents were out there, but the reporting was really low. Managers practiced speaking about and emphasizing the importance of their health and safety, and they created a safe environment for employees to report hazards and near misses. Their safety improved overall because people were paying attention to safety. It wasn't punitive anymore. The "safety for supervisors" training worked.

And what makes us so different is that all of our communication courses and leadership training always have a component of deliberate practice. I don't believe that a course without practice is very useful at all. It's just knowledge transfer, and it's missing the part where people try, fail, try again, and build their muscle memory through repetition. That's why most training out there isn't useful for our industry. We're people who learn by doing.

In the trades, where manual skills, judgment, and safety are your bread and butter, applying deliberate practice means your training needs to look different.

Instead of saying "do more installations," you're going to pick the challenging part of the installation, like complex piping geometry, and practice that part deliberately, on a sample, in the shop where it doesn't matter if someone makes a mistake.

Instead of letting a trainee do something wrong multiple times, you give immediate feedback on what they did well (keep doing that) and what needs correcting (let's not do that again). There's no point in letting someone do something wrong for a long time; it makes it harder to change the habit later.

You practice all the mini tasks within a larger procedure and have the trainee practice repeatedly until they become confident and reliable. You can do these mini tasks in a shop or as a sample, so mistakes don't cost much.

Instead of letting people stay comfortable, you stretch their skills and give them new things to try and learn so they grow faster. Keep pushing just beyond the comfort zone and give them stretch opportunities.

Instead of always correcting, draw attention and praise to progress. You can say, "On the last job, I checked for misalignment, and it was 12mm; now it's 3mm. That's an improvement, so let's keep practicing."

This is how you take a warm body fresh in the trade and get them upskilled and working capably much faster. The old "learning through osmosis" technique isn't going to close that decade-long mastery gap. Over time, these mini skills will add up to "common sense" to the point where someone will be able to handle non-standard scenarios.

At the heart of a strong learning ecosystem lies deliberate

practice—not just "do it again," but "do it better, and pay attention to how you improved." For tradespeople, that means structured repetition of the tricky bits, targeted feedback from a mentor, a safe learning environment, measurable improvement, and learning management software that helps you track all of the efforts.

When your framing, tools, mentorship, checklists, and learning system all support deliberate practice, you move from competent tradespeople to continuously improving experts.

CHAPTER 13

THE FUTURE IS NOW

THE FUTURE OF THE TRADES WILL NOT BE BUILT BY accident. It will be built by the people who show up, teach what they know, and commit to leaving the industry stronger than they found it. The truth is simple: every trade has survived because people took the time to show someone else how it's done. That hasn't changed. What has changed is the speed of the world around us and an education system that's failing to teach these skills. What's changed is our ability to rely on others to fix the problem for us. And the cost of doing nothing has changed. We can't afford to do things the same anymore.

You've seen the numbers. Retirements are accelerating. Work is piling up. Younger workers are entering the field with different expectations, different pressures, and different ways of learning. Artificial Intelligence is reshaping how information moves. Customers want faster work with fewer mistakes, and standards are high. Costs are even higher. No one is coming to save the trades unless the people in them take responsibility for passing the torch.

That's where you come in.

This might be the beginning of a new way of operating for you.

A new way of treating employees.

A new way of thinking about investing in people, leaders, and training.

A new way of understanding workplace culture.

I've been challenging the whole industry to think differently. I get that this feels daunting when you're the person who has to start doing something about it. That's the shitty thing about knowledge: Once you know it and believe it, you can't un-know it. Doing nothing feels wrong.

And if you've made it this far in the book, it's because you give a shit too.

Writing this book wasn't easy. I've never identified as a writer. I like my sleep. I'm not one to wake up at 4 a.m. and crank out a chapter before the family wakes up, but when I woke up in July 2025 with this book title and this message in my heart, I knew it needed to be written. That gut feeling, all of your stories, and the work I do with Boost are what brought this book to life.

I've done it because I care about this industry enough to get up early the same way many of you get up to drive to your shop, get on site, plan the day for your crews, do paperwork, order materials, and sort out staffing problems and headaches.

Since being a teenager at the dinner table and hearing the challenges my dad was having in his business, I've cared about the trades. When I brought my experience as a training professional into this industry, I realized most of you aren't going from 80 to 100 percent on this culture, training, and modernization journey. Most of you are right at the beginning.

And beginnings matter. Beginnings have teeth. (Yes, I had to look up what the spikes on a cog are called. Turns out "teeth" feels ironically accurate for this analogy.)

You are one of the teeth in the cogs of this industry. When too many teeth are broken, the chain falls off. We're a gritty bunch, and our impact on the industry does actually "have teeth."

So, let's get started. Let's do things a little differently:

- Let's choose not to lose the lifetime of experience held within the heads and hands of our senior tradespeople.
- Let's capture that knowledge and make it accessible for millennials, Gen Z, and the next generation currently in high school.
- Let's get organized and create effective training so we can be more productive and have a healthier bottom line.
- Let's retain people so we don't have constant churn.
- Let's help our leaders be the best they can be.

I'm proud of the work we're doing to make this happen for our clients. But I also know not all of you will be in a position to call us. So, I want you to be able to take this book and *do something* right away.

If I were a small company with a limited budget, here's where I'd start:

- I'd think about how I want to influence my culture — in whatever size business or team I lead.

- I'd get feedback from everybody who works with me and for me. I'd learn what they love about the work and what they don't, what they wish could be improved, and how their training and employee experience have been.
- I'd ask about their onboarding experience.
- I'd look at everyone's access to information. How it's organized, who can find what, and whether it supports the work or slows people down.
- I would listen. I would learn. And then I'd make a plan to do better.

Remember: things won't change overnight. Creating a learning ecosystem takes time, intention, and iteration. Nothing will be perfect the first time. You're going to start, build on the start, and iterate.

And for the future of the industry, I hope you get involved in recruiting young people into the trades. Maybe that means going to your local high school, joining your local association, participating in apprenticeship opportunities, or creating a great onboarding experience and recruitment strategy in your own business. I challenge you to take on apprentices and pour into them like your life depends on it—or at the very least, like your worker pipeline depends on it.

If I were you, I'd also look at how to improve myself as a leader. To recruit and retain great people, you've got to improve your own leadership and communication skills by taking a course, practicing, reading, and reflecting. You have to learn to lead yourself before expecting others to follow.

Shameless plug: check out our courses and services online.

We will strategize, practice with you, and help you future-proof your business. We're a "strategize and get shit done" partner . . . and we mean it.

And let me be clear about something: the next generation isn't "soft." They're overwhelmed. They're ambitious in different ways. They're hungry for someone to show them how the real world works. They want to learn. They want to contribute. They want to feel part of something worth sticking around for. They want to be led by someone who believes in the future—not someone who's bitter about the past.

The future is yours.

You're positioned beautifully to do something great for the industry.

And I want to be your accountability buddy. Email me at *Team@BoostLD.com* and tell me what action you're taking right now. If you need help, reach out.

Let's fucking go.

ABOUT THE AUTHOR

MANJA HORNER IS A THIRD-GENERATION tradesperson who grew up working in her family's restoration business, learning craft, precision, and pride of work from her father and the experienced masters who she worked alongside. She knows the rhythm of a job site, the weight of responsibility on a project, the culture and unspoken rules that shape life in the trades—because she's lived them.

But she didn't stop there. For more than sixteen years, Manja has built a career in skills training, leadership development, and curriculum design—working across nearly every industry. Today, she's back where her roots are: supporting skilled trades companies, unions, and frontline teams across North America as the founder of Boost Union and Boost Learning Design. She helps organizations strengthen their supervisors, modernize workforce practices, train workers, and build workplaces people want to stay in.

She has seen what's working. She has seen where the industry fails the next generation of workers. And she knows the cost of waiting. It's not too late—but it's close.

In Pass the Torch, Manja challenges owners and leaders to stop looking outward for solutions. No government program, trade school, or recruitment campaign will save a company that refuses to develop its own people. Her message is clear: build an irresistible workplace, train your leaders, capture your knowledge before it retires, and create your own workforce pipeline from the ground up. The future of the trades depends on it.